50% OFF Online Praxis Teaching Reading Elementary Education Prep Course!

Dear Customer,

We consider it an honor and a privilege that you chose our Praxis Teaching Reading Elementary Education Study Guide. As a way of showing our appreciation and to help us better serve you, we have partnered with Mometrix Test Preparation to offer you **50% off their online Praxis Teaching Reading Elementary Education Prep Course**. Many Praxis Teaching Reading Elementary Education courses are needlessly expensive and don't deliver enough value. With their course, you get access to the best Praxis Teaching Reading Elementary Education prep material, and **you only pay half price**.

Mometrix has structured their online course to perfectly complement your printed study guide. The Praxis Teaching Reading Prep Course contains **in-depth lessons** that cover all the most important topics, **40+ video reviews** that explain difficult concepts, over **250 practice questions** to ensure you feel prepared, and **330+ digital flashcards**, so you can study while you're on the go.

Online Praxis Teaching Reading Elementary Education Prep Course

Topics Included:
- Phonological and Phonemic Awareness
- Phonics and Decoding
- Vocabulary and Fluency
- Comprehension of Literacy and Informational Texts
- Writing
- Assessment and Instructional Decision Making

Course Features:
- Praxis 5205 Study Guide
    - Get content that complements our best-selling study guide.
- Full-Length Practice Tests
    - With over 250 practice questions, you can test yourself again and again.
- Mobile Friendly
    - If you need to study on the go, the course is easily accessible from your mobile device.
- Praxis Teaching Reading Flashcards
    - Our course includes a flashcard mode with over 330 content cards to help you study.

To receive this discount, visit them at mometrix.com/university/praxis5205 or simply scan this QR code with your smartphone. At the checkout page, enter the discount code: **5205TPB50**

If you have any questions or concerns, please contact Mometrix at support@mometrix.com.

Sincerely,

 in partnership with

FREE Test Taking Tips Video/DVD Offer

To better serve you, we created videos covering test taking tips that we want to give you for FREE. **These videos cover world-class tips that will help you succeed on your test.**

We just ask that you send us feedback about this product. Please let us know what you thought about it—whether good, bad, or indifferent.

To get your **FREE videos**, you can use the QR code below or email freevideos@studyguideteam.com with "Free Videos" in the subject line and the following information in the body of the email:

    a. The title of your product

    b. Your product rating on a scale of 1-5, with 5 being the highest

    c. Your feedback about the product

If you have any questions or concerns, please don't hesitate to contact us at info@studyguideteam.com.

Thank you!

Praxis Teaching Reading Elementary 5205 Study Guide

Test Prep and Practice Exam [2nd Edition]

Lydia Morrison

Copyright © 2024 by TPB Publishing

All rights reserved. No part of this publication may be reproduced, distributed, or transmitted in any form or by any means, including photocopying, recording, or other electronic or mechanical methods, without the prior written permission of the publisher, except in the case of brief quotations embodied in critical reviews and certain other noncommercial uses permitted by copyright law.

Written and edited by TPB Publishing.

TPB Publishing is not associated with or endorsed by any official testing organization. TPB Publishing is a publisher of unofficial educational products. All test and organization names are trademarks of their respective owners. Content in this book is included for utilitarian purposes only and does not constitute an endorsement by TPB Publishing of any particular point of view.

Interested in buying more than 10 copies of our product? Contact us about bulk discounts:
bulkorders@studyguideteam.com

ISBN 13: 9781637759752

Table of Contents

Welcome ---- 1
   FREE Videos/DVD OFFER ---- 1
Quick Overview ---- 2
Test-Taking Strategies ---- 3
Introduction ---- 7
Study Prep Plan ---- 9
Phonological & Phonemic Awareness Including Emergent Literacy ---- 12
   Practice Quiz ---- 18
   Answer Explanations ---- 19
Phonics and Decoding ---- 20
   Practice Quiz ---- 27
   Answer Explanations ---- 28
Vocabulary and Fluency ---- 29
   Practice Quiz ---- 38
   Answer Explanations ---- 39
Comprehension of Literary and Informational Text ---- 40
   Practice Quiz ---- 61
   Answer Explanations ---- 62
Written Expression ---- 63
   Spelling and Grammar ---- 68
Practice Test ---- 75
Assessment and Instructional Decision Making ---- 89
   Constructed Response Question ---- 90
   Sample Constructed Response Questions ---- 92
Answer Explanations ---- 94
Index ---- 104

Welcome

Dear Reader,

Welcome to your new Test Prep Books study guide! We are pleased that you chose us to help you prepare for your exam. There are many study options to choose from, and we appreciate you choosing us. Studying can be a daunting task, but we have designed a smart, effective study guide to help prepare you for what lies ahead.

Whether you're a parent helping your child learn and grow, a high school student working hard to get into your dream college, or a nursing student studying for a complex exam, we want to help give you the tools you need to succeed. We hope this study guide gives you the skills and the confidence to thrive, and we can't thank you enough for allowing us to be part of your journey.

In an effort to continue to improve our products, we welcome feedback from our customers. We look forward to hearing from you. Suggestions, success stories, and criticisms can all be communicated by emailing us at info@studyguideteam.com.

Sincerely,
Test Prep Books Team

FREE Videos/DVD OFFER

Doing well on your exam requires both knowing the test content and understanding how to use that knowledge to do well on the test. We offer completely FREE test taking tip videos. **These videos cover world-class tips that you can use to succeed on your test.**

To get your **FREE videos**, you can use the QR code below or email freevideos@studyguideteam.com with "Free Videos" in the subject line and the following information in the body of the email:

    a. The title of your product
    b. Your product rating on a scale of 1-5, with 5 being the highest
    c. Your feedback about the product

If you have any questions or concerns, please don't hesitate to contact us at info@studyguideteam.com.

Quick Overview

As you draw closer to taking your exam, effective preparation becomes more and more important. Thankfully, you have this study guide to help you get ready. Use this guide to help keep your studying on track and refer to it often.

This study guide contains several key sections that will help you be successful on your exam. The guide contains tips for what you should do the night before and the day of the test. Also included are test-taking tips. Knowing the right information is not always enough. Many well-prepared test takers struggle with exams. These tips will help equip you to accurately read, assess, and answer test questions.

A large part of the guide is devoted to showing you what content to expect on the exam and to helping you better understand that content. In this guide are practice test questions so that you can see how well you have grasped the content. Then, answer explanations are provided so that you can understand why you missed certain questions.

Don't try to cram the night before you take your exam. This is not a wise strategy for a few reasons. First, your retention of the information will be low. Your time would be better used by reviewing information you already know rather than trying to learn a lot of new information. Second, you will likely become stressed as you try to gain a large amount of knowledge in a short amount of time. Third, you will be depriving yourself of sleep. So be sure to go to bed at a reasonable time the night before. Being well-rested helps you focus and remain calm.

Be sure to eat a substantial breakfast the morning of the exam. If you are taking the exam in the afternoon, be sure to have a good lunch as well. Being hungry is distracting and can make it difficult to focus. You have hopefully spent lots of time preparing for the exam. Don't let an empty stomach get in the way of success!

When travelling to the testing center, leave earlier than needed. That way, you have a buffer in case you experience any delays. This will help you remain calm and will keep you from missing your appointment time at the testing center.

Be sure to pace yourself during the exam. Don't try to rush through the exam. There is no need to risk performing poorly on the exam just so you can leave the testing center early. Allow yourself to use all of the allotted time if needed.

Remain positive while taking the exam even if you feel like you are performing poorly. Thinking about the content you should have mastered will not help you perform better on the exam.

Once the exam is complete, take some time to relax. Even if you feel that you need to take the exam again, you will be well served by some down time before you begin studying again. It's often easier to convince yourself to study if you know that it will come with a reward!

Test-Taking Strategies

1. Predicting the Answer

When you feel confident in your preparation for a multiple-choice test, try predicting the answer before reading the answer choices. This is especially useful on questions that test objective factual knowledge. By predicting the answer before reading the available choices, you eliminate the possibility that you will be distracted or led astray by an incorrect answer choice. You will feel more confident in your selection if you read the question, predict the answer, and then find your prediction among the answer choices. After using this strategy, be sure to still read all of the answer choices carefully and completely. If you feel unprepared, you should not attempt to predict the answers. This would be a waste of time and an opportunity for your mind to wander in the wrong direction.

2. Reading the Whole Question

Too often, test takers scan a multiple-choice question, recognize a few familiar words, and immediately jump to the answer choices. Test authors are aware of this common impatience, and they will sometimes prey upon it. For instance, a test author might subtly turn the question into a negative, or he or she might redirect the focus of the question right at the end. The only way to avoid falling into these traps is to read the entirety of the question carefully before reading the answer choices.

3. Looking for Wrong Answers

Long and complicated multiple-choice questions can be intimidating. One way to simplify a difficult multiple-choice question is to eliminate all of the answer choices that are clearly wrong. In most sets of answers, there will be at least one selection that can be dismissed right away. If the test is administered on paper, the test taker could draw a line through it to indicate that it may be ignored; otherwise, the test taker will have to perform this operation mentally or on scratch paper. In either case, once the obviously incorrect answers have been eliminated, the remaining choices may be considered. Sometimes identifying the clearly wrong answers will give the test taker some information about the correct answer. For instance, if one of the remaining answer choices is a direct opposite of one of the eliminated answer choices, it may well be the correct answer. The opposite of obviously wrong is obviously right! Of course, this is not always the case. Some answers are obviously incorrect simply because they are irrelevant to the question being asked. Still, identifying and eliminating some incorrect answer choices is a good way to simplify a multiple-choice question.

4. Don't Overanalyze

Anxious test takers often overanalyze questions. When you are nervous, your brain will often run wild, causing you to make associations and discover clues that don't actually exist. If you feel that this may be a problem for you, do whatever you can to slow down during the test. Try taking a deep breath or counting to ten. As you read and consider the question, restrict yourself to the particular words used by the author. Avoid thought tangents about what the author *really* meant, or what he or she was *trying* to say. The only things that matter on a multiple-choice test are the words that are actually in the question. You must avoid reading too much into a multiple-choice question, or supposing that the writer meant something other than what he or she wrote.

5. No Need for Panic

It is wise to learn as many strategies as possible before taking a multiple-choice test, but it is likely that you will come across a few questions for which you simply don't know the answer. In this situation, avoid panicking. Because most multiple-choice tests include dozens of questions, the relative value of a single wrong answer is small. As much as possible, you should compartmentalize each question on a multiple-choice test. In other words, you should not allow your feelings about one question to affect your success on the others. When you find a question that you either don't understand or don't know how to answer, just take a deep breath and do your best. Read the entire question slowly and carefully. Try rephrasing the question a couple of different ways. Then, read all of the answer choices carefully. After eliminating obviously wrong answers, make a selection and move on to the next question.

6. Confusing Answer Choices

When working on a difficult multiple-choice question, there may be a tendency to focus on the answer choices that are the easiest to understand. Many people, whether consciously or not, gravitate to the answer choices that require the least concentration, knowledge, and memory. This is a mistake. When you come across an answer choice that is confusing, you should give it extra attention. A question might be confusing because you do not know the subject matter to which it refers. If this is the case, don't

eliminate the answer before you have affirmatively settled on another. When you come across an answer choice of this type, set it aside as you look at the remaining choices. If you can confidently assert that one of the other choices is correct, you can leave the confusing answer aside. Otherwise, you will need to take a moment to try to better understand the confusing answer choice. Rephrasing is one way to tease out the sense of a confusing answer choice.

7. Your First Instinct

Many people struggle with multiple-choice tests because they overthink the questions. If you have studied sufficiently for the test, you should be prepared to trust your first instinct once you have carefully and completely read the question and all of the answer choices. There is a great deal of research suggesting that the mind can come to the correct conclusion very quickly once it has obtained all of the relevant information. At times, it may seem to you as if your intuition is working faster even than your reasoning mind. This may in fact be true. The knowledge you obtain while studying may be retrieved from your subconscious before you have a chance to work out the associations that support it. Verify your instinct by working out the reasons that it should be trusted.

8. Key Words

Many test takers struggle with multiple-choice questions because they have poor reading comprehension skills. Quickly reading and understanding a multiple-choice question requires a mixture of skill and experience. To help with this, try jotting down a few key words and phrases on a piece of scrap paper. Doing this concentrates the process of reading and forces the mind to weigh the relative importance of the question's parts. In selecting words and phrases to write down, the test taker thinks

Test-Taking Strategies

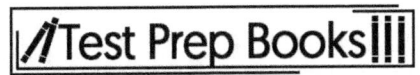

about the question more deeply and carefully. This is especially true for multiple-choice questions that are preceded by a long prompt.

9. Subtle Negatives

One of the oldest tricks in the multiple-choice test writer's book is to subtly reverse the meaning of a question with a word like *not* or *except*. If you are not paying attention to each word in the question, you can easily be led astray by this trick. For instance, a common question format is, "Which of the following is…?" Obviously, if the question instead is, "Which of the following is not…?," then the answer will be quite different. Even worse, the test makers are aware of the potential for this mistake and will include one answer choice that would be correct if the question were not negated or reversed. A test taker who misses the reversal will find what he or she believes to be a correct answer and will be so confident that he or she will fail to reread the question and discover the original error. The only way to avoid this is to practice a wide variety of multiple-choice questions and to pay close attention to each and every word.

10. Reading Every Answer Choice

It may seem obvious, but you should always read every one of the answer choices! Too many test takers fall into the habit of scanning the question and assuming that they understand the question because they recognize a few key words. From there, they pick the first answer choice that answers the question they believe they have read. Test takers who read all of the answer choices might discover that one of the latter answer choices is actually *more* correct. Moreover, reading all of the answer choices can remind you of facts related to the question that can help you arrive at the correct answer. Sometimes, a misstatement or incorrect detail in one of the latter answer choices will trigger your memory of the subject and will enable you to find the right answer. Failing to read all of the answer choices is like not reading all of the items on a restaurant menu: you might miss out on the perfect choice.

11. Spot the Hedges

One of the keys to success on multiple-choice tests is paying close attention to every word. This is never truer than with words like *almost*, *most*, *some*, and *sometimes*. These words are called "hedges" because they indicate that a statement is not totally true or not true in every place and time. An absolute statement will contain no hedges, but in many subjects, the answers are not always straightforward or absolute. There are always exceptions to the rules in these subjects. For this reason,

you should favor those multiple-choice questions that contain hedging language. The presence of qualifying words indicates that the author is taking special care with his or her words, which is certainly important when composing the right answer. After all, there are many ways to be wrong, but there is only one way to be right! For this reason, it is wise to avoid answers that are absolute when taking a multiple-choice test. An absolute answer is one that says things are either all one way or all another. They often include words like *every*, *always*, *best*, and *never*. If you are taking a multiple-choice test in a subject that doesn't lend itself to absolute answers, be on your guard if you see any of these words.

12. Long Answers

In many subject areas, the answers are not simple. As already mentioned, the right answer often requires hedges. Another common feature of the answers to a complex or subjective question are qualifying clauses, which are groups of words that subtly modify the meaning of the sentence. If the question or answer choice describes a rule to which there are exceptions or the subject matter is complicated, ambiguous, or confusing, the correct answer will require many words in order to be expressed clearly and accurately. In essence, you should not be deterred by answer choices that seem excessively long. Oftentimes, the author of the text will not be able to write the correct answer without offering some qualifications and modifications. Your job is to read the answer choices thoroughly and completely and to select the one that most accurately and precisely answers the question.

13. Restating to Understand

Sometimes, a question on a multiple-choice test is difficult not because of what it asks but because of how it is written. If this is the case, restate the question or answer choice in different words. This process serves a couple of important purposes. First, it forces you to concentrate on the core of the question. In order to rephrase the question accurately, you have to understand it well. Rephrasing the question will concentrate your mind on the key words and ideas. Second, it will present the information to your mind in a fresh way. This process may trigger your memory and render some useful scrap of information picked up while studying.

14. True Statements

Sometimes an answer choice will be true in itself, but it does not answer the question. This is one of the main reasons why it is essential to read the question carefully and completely before proceeding to the answer choices. Too often, test takers skip ahead to the answer choices and look for true statements. Having found one of these, they are content to select it without reference to the question above. The savvy test taker will always read the entire question before turning to the answer choices. Then, having settled on a correct answer choice, he or she will refer to the original question and ensure that the selected answer is relevant. The mistake of choosing a correct-but-irrelevant answer choice is especially common on questions related to specific pieces of objective knowledge.

15. No Patterns

One of the more dangerous ideas that circulates about multiple-choice tests is that the correct answers tend to fall into patterns. These erroneous ideas range from a belief that B and C are the most common right answers, to the idea that an unprepared test-taker should answer "A-B-A-C-A-D-A-B-A." It cannot be emphasized enough that pattern-seeking of this type is exactly the WRONG way to approach a multiple choice test. To begin with, it is highly unlikely that the test maker will plot the correct answers according to some predetermined pattern. The questions are scrambled and delivered in a random order. Furthermore, even if the test maker was following a pattern in the assignation of correct answers, there is no reason why the test taker would know which pattern he or she was using. Any attempt to discern a pattern in the answer choices is a waste of time and a distraction from the real work of taking the test. A test taker would be much better served by extra preparation before the test than by reliance on a pattern in the answers.

Introduction

Function of the Test

The Praxis Teaching Reading: Elementary Education Exam is for students or professionals entering or completing teacher preparation programs. This exam measures the ability of an individual to teach oral language and reading development at an elementary level. As identified by the National Reading Panel, it covers the five most important aspects of teaching reading instruction: phonemic awareness, phonics, fluency, vocabulary, and comprehension. This exam is offered nationwide through a variety of testing locations. The number of people who took the Praxis Teaching Reading Exam in the 2019-2020 year was 2,851.

Test Administration

The Praxis Teaching Reading Exam is available for test takers each day of each month, whether testing in-person or remote, as of 2022. You can register to take the exam on the ETS Praxis website, and an available listing of test sites will be available for you to choose from. Retesting is available once every 28 days, or after 28 days for subject tests. Praxis tests are offered through the Educational Testing Service (ETS), and ETS provides accommodations to persons who have disabilities. Some accommodations should be requested, so visit the ETS website to find out more.

Test Format

The testing room prohibits cell phone use, and you are not allowed to bring in personal items, beverages, study materials, pencils, pens, calculators, or any electronic device of any kind. Personal items are not allowed in the test room, so if your facility does not provide storage, you must plan accordingly.

The Praxis Teaching Reading Exam is a 150-minute test with 90 selected-response questions and 3 constructed-response questions.

The table below shows a breakdown of the content domains:

Content Category	Number of Questions	Percentage of Exam
• Phonological and Phonemic Awareness and Emergent Literacy	14	11%
• Phonics and Decoding	18	15%
• Vocabulary and Fluency	21	18%
• Comprehension of Literary and Informational Text	21	18%
• Written Expression	16	13%
• Assessment and Instructional Decision Making (Constructed Response)	3	25%

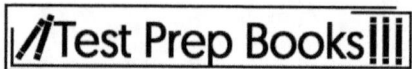

Scoring

The passing score for the Praxis Teaching Reading Exam depends on each particular state's requirements. You will be notified of a passing score after you take the exam and your states have been entered into the system. A list of states and passing scores are also available on the ETS website. The highest score of any other Praxis tests you have taken in the past ten years will show up on your score report along with your new score. End scores reveal how you did in each content, so if you choose to retake the exam, you will know which areas to focus on the most. All scores for Praxis exams are valid for ten years.

Recent/Future Developments

Praxis exams are updated on a regular basis to align with new core content. Test scores, however, will be valid for a ten-year period regardless of whether or not the content is still relevant.

Study Prep Plan

1 **Schedule** - Use one of our study schedules below or come up with one of your own.

2 **Relax** - Test anxiety can hurt even the best students. There are many ways to reduce stress. Find the one that works best for you.

3 **Execute** - Once you have a good plan in place, be sure to stick to it.

One Week Study Schedule		
Day 1	Phonological & Phonemic Awareness Including Emergent Literacy	
Day 2	Vocabulary and Fluency	
Day 3	Comprehension of Literary and Informational Text	
Day 4	Literary Devices	
Day 5	Written Expression	
Day 6	Practice Test	
Day 7	Take Your Exam!	

Two Week Study Schedule				
Day 1	Phonological & Phonemic Awareness...	Day 8	Differentiating Instruction, Tasks...
Day 2	Instructional Methods to Teach Beginning...	Day 9	Literary Devices
Day 3	Phonics and Decoding	Day 10	Using Technology to Support Students
Day 4	Syllable Types in Decoding Multisyllabic...	Day 11	Written Expression
Day 5	Vocabulary and Fluency	Day 12	Spelling and Grammar
Day 6	Teaching Word Solving	Day 13	Practice Test
Day 7	Comprehension of Literary...	Day 14	Take Your Exam!

Build your own prep plan by visiting:

testprepbooks.com/prep

As you study for your test, we'd like to take the opportunity to remind you that you are capable of great things! With the right tools and dedication, you truly can do anything you set your mind to. The fact that you are holding this book right now shows how committed you are. In case no one has told you lately, you've got this! Our intention behind including this coloring page is to give you the chance to take some time to engage your creative side when you need a little brain-break from studying. As a company, we want to encourage people like you to achieve their dreams by providing good quality study materials for the tests and certifications that improve careers and change lives. As individuals, many of us have taken such tests in our careers, and we know how challenging this process can be. While we can't come alongside you and cheer you on personally, we can offer you the space to recall your purpose, reconnect with your passion, and refresh your brain through an artistic practice. We wish you every success, and happy studying!

Phonological & Phonemic Awareness Including Emergent Literacy

Instructional Methods for Teaching Phonological Awareness

Phonological awareness is the understanding that words are made up of multiple sounds working together. These word sounds may be distinguishable by syllables, onsets and rimes, or by phonemes. Teachers can assess for students' phonological awareness by asking them to break words into multiple parts, by having students select rhyming words from a list, or by giving students a series of sounds and asking them what word the sounds form.

Recognition of Rhyme and Alliteration
Teaching a child to recognize **rhymes** within words is one of the basic levels of phonological awareness. A child must closely pay attention to the word's different sounds. By teaching them to pay attention to the individual sounds, children also learn that words can be made up of multiple, different parts. They should listen to the sounds within different words and determine if they are similar, meaning they have rhyme, or if they are different, meaning they do not have rhyme.

Alliteration is when two or more words in a phrase begin with the same sound or sound group. For example, the phrase *chunky chocolate chips* includes the 'ch' sound at the beginning of each word.

Teaching a child to recognize alliteration in words is similar to teaching them to recognize rhyme. Not only is it another early, basic level of phonological awareness, but it helps the child to recognize patterns within words. Having children listen to the individual word sounds helps reinforce that words are broken up into multiple parts.

Segmenting
When a child recognizes that there are multiple parts of a word and that the word can be broken down into its different sounds, they naturally begin **segmenting** the phonemes in the word. Segmenting is the ability to break words into their individual, specific sounds. For example, a child might break the word "cat" into its individual sounds: /k/ /a/ /t/.

Teachers can support segmenting through the use of Elkonin boxes or sound boxes, which help students learn to segment words into individual sounds. Elkonin boxes are easy to create, simply requiring the teacher to draw a box for each sound in a word. For the example "cat", the teacher would draw three boxes. Then, as the teacher says each sound in the word "cat", the students will either write or place a pre-created letter block in each box to represent the sounds in the word ("c" "a" "t").

Blending
Blending is essentially the inversion of segmenting. Rather than being presented with the whole word, the child is first presented with the individual sounds of a word and is then asked to "blend" them together to make the intended word. For example, a student might be given the sounds: /k/ /a/ /t/. If the child were to put these sounds together, they would form the word "cat".

Manipulation of Syllables
As students develop their phonological awareness, they may begin manipulating the syllables within words. The **manipulation of syllables** refers to a child "playing" with word sounds to create new words.

For example, a student may be given the word "cat" and asked to change the /c/ to a /b/ in order to create a new word. The students would respond that the new word is "bat".

Onset and Rime
Onset refers to the consonants that occur before a vowel. It is the initial phonological piece of any word. **Rime** refers to the letters that follow after the onset. For example, in the word "cat," the "c" would be the onset, and "at" would be the rime.

Instructional Methods for Teaching Phonemic Awareness

Phonemic Awareness in Reading Development
A **phoneme** is the smallest unit of sound in a given language. Understanding phonemes is one of the many skills associated with phonemic awareness. A child demonstrates phonemic awareness when identifying rhymes, recognizing alliterations, and isolating specific sounds inside a word or a set of words. Students who demonstrate basic **phonemic awareness** will eventually also be able to blend together a variety of phonemes independently and appropriately.

Some classroom strategies to strengthen phonemic awareness may include:

- Introduction to nursery rhymes and word play
- Introduction to speech discrimination techniques to train the ear to hear more accurately
- Repeated instruction connecting sounds to letters and blending sounds
- Use of visual images coupled with corresponding sounds and words
- Teaching speech sounds through direct instruction
- Comparing known to unfamiliar words
- Practicing pronunciation of newly introduced letters, letter combinations, and words
- Practicing word decoding
- Differentiating similar sounding words

Development of Phonemic-Awareness Skills
Age-appropriate and developmentally appropriate instruction for phonological and phonemic awareness is key to helping children strengthen their reading and writing skills. Phonological and phonemic awareness (PPA) instruction works to enhance correct speech, improve understanding and application of accurate letter-to-sound correspondence, and strengthen spelling skills. Since skill-building involving phonemes is not a natural process, PPA instruction is especially important for children who have limited access and exposure to reading materials and who lack familial encouragement to read. Strategies that educators can implement include leading word and sound games, focusing on phoneme skill-building activities, and ensuring all activities focus on the fun, playful nature of words and sounds instead of rote memorization and drilling techniques.

Deletion
Phoneme deletion promotes the development of a child's phonemic awareness, which is part of developing their overall phonological awareness. Deletion involves having students take a word and delete a specific phoneme to create a new word. For example, a student might start with the word "groundhog". The teacher may ask the student to say the word without "hog". The student would say "ground."

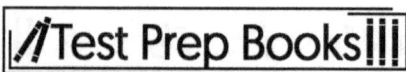

Phonological & Phonemic Awareness Including Emergent Literacy

Teachers can also use visual aids to assist in teaching phoneme deletion. For example, the teacher can use colored tiles with phonemes written on them to represent a word (example: "ch" and "air" to spell "chair"). Then, the teacher can remove one tile ("ch") and ask students to say what the other tile says ("air"). This helps both visual learners and students who have trouble understanding phoneme deletion.

Substitution

Phoneme substitution, like phoneme deletion, helps to develop a child's phonemic and phonological awareness. Substitution is when a student takes a word and substitutes certain phonemes within the word with other phonemes, creating a new word. We looked at an example of this earlier. Take the word "cat." Substitute the /k/ sound (phoneme) with the /b/ sound (phoneme). In doing so, you get a new word, "bat." Substitution, like deletion, is another way for a child to manipulate and show mastery of language and literacy.

Develop Student's Expressive and Receptive Language Skills

English language skills can be broken down into two categories: expressive (talking skills) and receptive (listening skills). Students need different types of encouragement at every stage to develop their language skills.

Receptive language is defined as when students are able to understand words and can begin to follow instructions but aren't necessarily able to use words to communicate yet. Educators can encourage this stage in literacy development by providing the student with many opportunities to interact on a social level with peers. Educators should also consider starting a personal dictionary, introducing word flashcards, and providing the student with opportunities to listen to a story read by another peer, or as a computer-based activity. One of the simplest and best ways to develop receptive language skills is through reading aloud to students and asking basic comprehension questions.

Expressive language is defined as when students can express themselves with either words or gestures. It often comes after a solid understanding of receptive language. There are many ways to build upon expressive language, which vary depending on the child's literacy level.

When a child begins to communicate to express a need or attempt to ask or respond to a question, the child is said to be at the early intermediate literacy stage. Educators should continue to build vocabulary knowledge and introduce activities that require the student to complete the endings of sentences, fill in the blanks, and describe the beginning or ending of familiar stories.

When a child begins to demonstrate comprehension of more complex vocabulary and abstract ideas, the child is advancing into the intermediate literacy stage. It is at this stage that children are able to challenge themselves to meet the classroom learning expectations and start to use their newly acquired literacy skills to read, write, listen, and speak. Educators may consider providing students with more advanced reading opportunities, such as partner-shared reading, silent reading, and choral reading.

When a child is able to apply literacy skills to learn new information across many subjects, the child is progressing toward the early advanced literacy stage. The child can now tackle complex literacy tasks and confidently handle much more cognitively demanding material. To strengthen reading comprehension, educators should consider the introduction to word webs and semantic organizers. Book reports and class presentations, as well as continued opportunities to access a variety of reading material, will help to strengthen the child's newly acquired literacy skills.

Instructional Methods to Teach Beginning Readers Concepts about Print

Concepts of Print

Print awareness includes the understanding that:

1. **Words** are made of letters, spaces appear between words, and words make sentences.

2. **Print** is organized in a particular way (e.g., read from left to right and top to bottom, read from front to back, etc.), so books must be tracked and held accordingly.

3. Different types of print serve specific purposes (magazines, billboards, essays, fiction, etc.).

Print awareness provides the foundation on which all other literacy skills are built. It is often the first stage of reading development. Print awareness helps students develop skills such as word reading, reading comprehension, and letter-sound correspondence. For this reason, a child's performance on tasks relevant to their print awareness is indicative of the child's future reading achievement.

The following strategies can be used to increase print awareness in students:

1. *A teacher can read aloud to students or conduct shared reading experiences.* In order to maximize print awareness within the student, the reader should point out the form, function, orientation, and sounds of letters and words.

2. *Utilize shared reading experiences as a tool for building one-to-one correspondence.* **One-to-one correspondence** is the ability to match written letters or words to a spoken word when reading. This can be accomplished by pointing to words as they are read. This helps students make text-to-word connections. Pointing also aids **directionality**, or the ability to track the words that are being read.

3. *Use the child's environment.* To reinforce print awareness, teachers can make a child aware of print in their environment, such as words on traffic signs. Teachers can reinforce this by labeling objects in the classroom.

4. *Instruct students about book organization during read-alouds.* Students should be taught the proper orientation, tracking, and numbering conventions of books. For example, teachers can differentiate the title from the author's name on the front cover of a book.

5. *Let students practice.* Allowing students to practice book-handling skills with wordless books, predictable text, or patterned text will help to instill print awareness.

Return Sweep

Return sweeping refers to a reader moving their eyes from the end of one line on the right side of the page back to the left side of the page to begin a new line. The return sweep can be taught by modeling pointing to the words when reading to your child. Your child will learn to do this as they begin reading independently, and physically moving their finger from the end of one sentence to the beginning of the next will help train their eyes to follow this same process.

Phonological & Phonemic Awareness Including Emergent Literacy

Parts of a Book

It is important to teach a new reader the different parts of a book, as each part contains its own valid and useful information. While there are simpler ways to reduce this list, here is an extensive list of the different parts/components of a standard book.

(1) Front Matter

    (a) Title

    (b) Copyright information

    (c) Dedication (if applicable)

    (d) Table of Contents

    (e) Foreword (if applicable)

    (f) Acknowledgments

    (g) Preface or Introduction (if applicable)

    (h) Prologue (if applicable)

(2) Body Matter

    (a) This is the content of the book

(3) Back Matter

    (a) Epilogue (if applicable)

    (b) Appendix (if applicable)

    (c) Glossary (if applicable)

    (d) Bibliography (if applicable)

    (e) Index (if applicable)

    (f) Author's biography

The Form and Function of Print

Fostering print awareness also entails making sure the reader understands what books are used for and how a book actually works. This means that the reader needs to know how to turn a page, how to navigate the page (numbers and chapters), and how to distinguish the different parts of the book.

Included in this is also making sure the reader knows that print is typically organized from left to right and that there should be spaces between words. In order to help a new reader develop stronger print awareness and understanding of the form and function of print, environmental intervention is necessary. This means that parents and peers and any other influential members in the reader's life should make it a point to point out print. They should not only point out print but also make it a point to point out the different forms within print (i.e. line spacing, capitalization, page layouts, etc.)

Phonological & Phonemic Awareness Including Emergent Literacy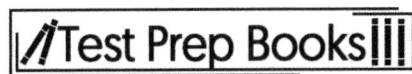

Identifying Upper-and Lowercase Letters in Various Fonts

Recognizing Uppercase and Lowercase Letters

Among the skills that are used to determine reading readiness, letter identification is the strongest predictor. **Letter recognition** is the identification of each letter in the alphabet. Letter recognition does not include letter-sound correspondences; however, learning about and being able to recognize letters may increase student motivation to learn letter sounds. Also, the names of many letters are similar to their sounds, so letter recognition serves as a gateway for the letter-sound relationships that are needed for reading to occur. Similarly, the ability to differentiate between uppercase and lowercase letters is beneficial in determining where a sentence begins and ends.

To be fluent in letter identification, students should be able to identify letter names in and out of context with automaticity. In order to obtain such familiarity with the identification of letters, students need ample experience, acquaintance, and practice with letters. Explicit instruction in letter recognition, practice printing uppercase and lowercase letters of the alphabet, and consistent exposure to printed letters are essential in the instruction of letter recognition.

Research has revealed that the following sequencing guidelines are necessary to effectively promote letter naming and identification:

1. The initial stage includes visual discrimination of shapes and curved lines.

2. Once students are able to identify and discriminate shapes with ease, then letter formations can be introduced. During the introduction of letter shapes, two letters that share visual (*p* and *q*) or auditory (/a/ and /u/) similarities should never be presented in back-to-back.

3. Next, uppercase letters are introduced. Uppercase letters are introduced before lowercase letters because they are easier to discriminate visually than lowercase letters. When letter formations are first presented to a student, their visual system analyzes the vertical, horizontal, and curved orientations of the letters. Therefore, teachers should use think-alouds when instructing how to write the shape of each letter. During think-alouds, teachers verbalize their own thought processes that occur when writing each part of a given letter. Students should be encouraged to do likewise when practicing printing the letters. Continuous consonant sounds and vowel sounds (like /s/, /a/, and /f/) should be taught before stop consonant sounds (like /t/, /p/, and /k/). Short vowel sounds should be taught before long vowel sounds.

4. Once uppercase letters are mastered, lowercase letters can be introduced. High-frequency lowercase letters (*a, e, t*) are introduced prior to low-frequency lowercase letters (*q, x, z*).

5. Once the recognition of letters is mastered, students need ample time manipulating and utilizing the letters. This can be done through sorting, matching, comparing, and writing activities.

Practice Quiz

1. Which of the following parts of a book could help a reader to find a specific word or concept they are looking for?
    a. Bibliography
    b. Appendix
    c. Preface
    d. Glossary

2. A student can say a few letters, can name animals and make animal sounds, but holds a book upside down. What area of reading is the student struggling in?
    a. Phonemic awareness
    b. Phonological awareness
    c. Print awareness
    d. Phoneme-grapheme correspondence

3. A teacher gives a group of students the word "can" and asks them to come up with rhyming words. The students respond with "ban", "tan" and "fan". Which of the following methods did they MOST LIKELY use to come up with their answer?
    a. Blending
    b. Substitution
    c. Deletion
    d. Decoding

4. In the word "tap", the "t" is considered the:
    a. Onset
    b. Rime
    c. Blend
    d. Segment

5. What is a phoneme?
    a. A word
    b. A relationship between a letter and a sound
    c. An individual sound
    d. A consonant

See answers on the next page

Answer Explanations

1. D: The glossary of a book is the best place to look for specific words and concepts. The appendix, bibliography, and preface of a book all serve other purposes than helping the reader look up specific words.

2. C: The student doesn't understand print awareness because they are holding the book upside down. Print awareness is an understanding of how books and other print work, meaning that books should be held in the correct direction, print should be read left to right, and the reader should know how to turn pages.

3. B: The students used substitution to come up with the rhyming words because they substituted the first letter "c" for other letters ("b", "t," and "f").

4. A: In the word "tap", the "t" is considered the onset (or initial consonant sound) and the "ap" is the rime (the letters that follow the onset).

5. C: A phoneme is the smallest unit of sound (for example, the phonogram "ph" represents the phoneme /f/). Choice A, a word, is typically composed of multiple phonemes. Choice B refers to phonics, and Choice D is a subtype of phoneme.

Phonics and Decoding

Teaching Phoneme-Grapheme Correspondence

Phoneme-grapheme correspondence or the **alphabetic principle** refers to a child's ability to recognize the correspondence between letter sounds (phoneme) and the visual representation of that letter (grapheme).

Some techniques for teaching phoneme-grapheme correspondence include:

- The teacher could say the phoneme and have the student write the grapheme, either in the air or on paper. Prior to the student being able to write, the teacher could say the phoneme and the student could just identify the grapheme from a small group of letters.
- The teacher could have the student choose a graphic from a set of images that begins with the same sound said by the teacher.
- The teacher can write a word, choose a letter sound, and ask the student to identify the matching grapheme. For example, a teacher can ask "Where is the /c/ in cat?" and have the student point to the letter C.
- The teacher can point out the visual features of letters, like the curves and lines that students can use to help identify the letter, while saying the phonemic sound associated with it.

Teaching Phonics Systematically, Explicitly, and Recursively

Teaching phonics **systematically** simply means that phonics instruction is built gradually, one phonics sound at a time. It provides a structure for teaching phonics in an orderly, step-by-by step approach that starts at the basics and builds upon student knowledge with each new skill. Systematic instruction also involves plenty of review to ensure that students don't forget previous phonics knowledge and skills. In systematic phonics instruction, it's important that the teacher focuses on one letter-sound at a time, waiting until students master each sound to move forward to the next.

Teaching phonics **explicitly** means that each part of the lesson is teacher-led and modeled to ensure that students are taught phonics in an accurate and detailed way. The teacher leads every part of the lesson and does not expect for students to simply learn letter sounds through reading or other methods. Explicit phonics instruction involves repetition, direct instruction, and consistency. A teacher who teaches phonics explicitly might do so by writing the letter B on the board and saying, "B says /b/ as in bin, bee, and bat". The students then look at the B and chorus the /b/ sound.

Teaching phonics systematically and explicitly has been proven, through research, to be more effective than teaching phonics implicitly, or **recursively**. Implicit phonics focuses on teaching from the whole word to its parts, rather than from its parts to the whole word, as done with explicit phonics. It is more student-led, requiring the student to use context to try and figure out what a word might be, rather than using the part-to-whole approach of sounding it out.

Teaching Common Phonics Patterns and Rules

Decoding and encoding are **reciprocal phonological skills**, meaning that their steps are opposite of each other.

Phonics and Decoding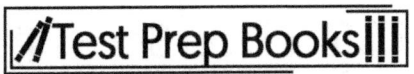

Decoding is the application of letter-sound correspondences, letter patterns, and other phonics relationships that help students read and correctly pronounce words. Decoding helps students to recognize and read words quickly, increasing reading fluency and comprehension. The steps of the decoding process are as follows:

1. The student identifies a written letter or letter combination.

2. The student identifies the sound of that letter or letter combination.

3. The student understands how the word's different letters or letter combinations fit together.

4. The student verbally blends the letter and letter combinations together to form a word.

Encoding is the spelling of words. In order to properly spell words, students must be familiar with letter/sound correspondences. Students must be able to put together phonemes, digraphs or blends, morphological units, consonant/vowel patterns, etc. The steps of encoding are identified below:

1. The student understands that letters and sounds make up words.

2. The student segments the sound parts of a word.

3. The student identifies the letter or letter combinations that correspond to each sound part.

4. The student then writes the letters and letter combinations in order to create the word.

Because the stages of decoding and encoding are reciprocal skills, phonics knowledge supports the development of reading and spelling. Likewise, the development of spelling skills reinforces phonics and decoding. In fact, the foundation of all good spelling programs is alignment with reading instruction and students' reading levels. Phonics instruction begins with simple syllable patterns and then progresses toward more complex patterns, the sounds of morphemes, and strategies for decoding multisyllabic words. Through this process, new vocabulary is developed. Sight word instruction should not begin until students are able to decode target words with automaticity and accuracy. Spelling is the last instructional component to be introduced.

After students master letter-sound correspondences, consonant sounds, and short vowel sounds, they should begin learning VC and CVC words. After mastery of VC and CVC words, students should learn consonant blends and digraphs, including CCVC words. Then, students should learn long vowel sounds, including CVCV words, followed by diphthongs.

Consonant Digraphs
Consonant digraphs are simply two or more consonants put together to represent a single sound. For example, in the word "tough," the "g" and "h" form "-gh," which can represent the sound /f/. A similar example would be the "p" and "h" in "digraph," also representing the sound /f/. Some other common consonant digraphs include: *ch, ck, kn, mb, ng, sh, th, wh,* and *wr*.

A teacher should introduce digraphs after students have mastered CVC words. Teachers should first introduce the concept of digraphs by explaining to students that a digraph is when two letters work together to make a single sound. Then, show examples of the digraph or digraphs they are first introducing, for example /ch/ and /sh/. Explain the letters C and H make the /ch/ sound, like in the word *chip*, and that the letters S and H make the /sh/ sound, like in the word *ship*. Break words into parts to identify the digraph, for example, the word chop can be broken into /ch/ /o/ /p/, students should then be able to identify the /ch/ sound as the digraph.

Blends

A **consonant blend** is similar to a consonant digraph in that it involves two or more consonants put together. However, blends are different than digraphs in that each consonant that is "blended" still has its own sound, they don't make a new sound like a digraph does. For example, think of the "s" and "t" in "star." Or you could think of the "c" and "l" in "clock". In this example, the "c" and "k" at the end would be an example of a consonant digraph as opposed to the "c" and "l" at the beginning which are a consonant blend.

Like digraphs, consonant blends can be taught after mastery of CVC words and should be taught explicitly, with many examples provided. It's important to note the most common consonant blends, which are s-blends, l-blends, and r-blends. S-blends are consonant blends that start with the letter "s", which can be at the beginning (e.g., space) or ending (e.g., mist) of a word. L-blends and r-blends include either an "l" or "r" as the second letter of the blend (e.g., place, slice, frown, and frost).

Diphthongs

A diphthong is formed when two vowel sounds combine to form a single syllable. There are eight diphthongs within the English language, examples of which are listed below. It's generally best to teach diphthongs after mastery of CVC words, blends, and digraphs.

Diphthong	Example	Diphthong	Example
"aw"	Straw, claw, law, saw, crawl	"au"	Haul, author, cause, pause, sauce
"ew"	Chew, blew, few, new, stew	"oo"	Food, shampoo, soon, room, balloon
"oi"	Point, join, coin, noise, spoil	"oy"	Boy, toy, joy, deploy, oyster
"ow"	Cow, how, brown, crown, flower	"ou"	House, cloud, round, ouch, found

Teachers should explicitly teach all eight diphthongs and have students practice identifying them within words. One great way to have students practice is by pairing cards that have pictures (e.g. moon, spoon, food) with a card that has that diphthong listed ("oo").

Schwa Sound

The **schwa** sound is a sound that any vowel could make. The simplest way to characterize the schwa sound is to say that the vowel is making the short /u/ sound, or the /ŭ/ sound. This would sound like "uh." For example, words like *above*, *camel*, and *freedom* contain the short /u/ sound. In *above*, the "a" and the "o" make the schwa sound. In *camel*, the "e" makes the sound. In *freedom*, the "o" makes the sound.

Phonics and Decoding

Word Families

Word families are words that share the same pattern or feature. This could look like the same combinations or letters and/or having similar sounds. See the chart below for a representation of word families.

ake	ate	ick	est	ay	ight	ing	ock	uck	ice
awake	create	sick	best	away	light	bring	clock	duck	dice
brake	date	chick	rest	day	fight	swing	block	yuck	mice
make	late	kick	test	clay	night	ring	knock	truck	nice
snake	mate	lick	vest	okay	right	sting	shock	tuck	slice
rake	skate	trick	nest	play	sight	spring	dock	chuck	twice

Teaching word families helps students to learn to spell words and furthers their connection of letters and sounds. By learning familiar word families, students can identify new words more easily because of their understanding of sounds. The best way to explain word families is to start simple (e.g., -at, -an, -it) and increase the difficulty as students' progress.

Morphological Analysis

Affixes

An **affix** is a letter or group of letters that can be added to a root word in order to change its meaning. There are **prefixes**, which are affixes added to the beginning of words; and there are **suffixes**, which are affixes added to the end of words. For example, in the word *transportable*, *-able* is the suffix.

Roots

The **root word** is the basic, original, and primary form of a word—what you get when you strip away the affixes. For example, in the word *transportable, port* would be the root word. It is the most basic and primary word inside the word *transportable*.

Base Words

Base words are very similar to root words. In fact, they are nearly indistinguishable. However, a base word is the word that can stand on its own. This is different from root words because not all root words are readable on their own. For example, in the word *transportable, transport* is the base word. It is not the root word because it is not simplified to the most basic and original form, however, it does still contain its meaning.

To teach affixes, roots, and base words, the concepts should be explained together in one lesson because they work together. Like the word *transportable*, the teacher can identify a few other words that have affixes, root, and base words. It's best to choose words that have different root and base words to help students understand the difference between the two.

To practice affixes, teachers can have students identify and underline the prefixes or suffixes within a given list of words. To practice root words, teachers can have students identify the meaning of the root word and come up with a few examples of words in which it appears, (e.g., the root word *port* means 'to carry' and can be found in *export, support,* and *portable*).

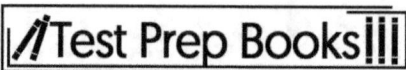

Syllable Types in Decoding Multisyllabic Words

Word-Analysis Skills

Phonics and decoding skills aid the analysis of new words. **Word analysis** is the ability to recognize the relationships between the spelling, syllabication, and pronunciation of new and/or unfamiliar words. Having a clear understanding of word structure and the meaning of morphemes aids in the analysis of new words.

However, not all words follow predictable patterns of phonics, morphology, or orthography. Such irregular words must be committed to memory and are called **sight words**.

Phonics skills, syllabic skills, structural analysis, word analysis, and memorization of sight words lead to word recognition automaticity. **Word recognition** is the ability to correctly and automatically recognize words in or out of context. Word recognition is a prerequisite for fluent reading and reading comprehension.

Reading Multisyllabic Words by Using Syllabication and Structural Analysis

Structural analysis is a word recognition skill that focuses on the meaning of word parts, or morphemes, during the introduction of a new word. Therefore, the instruction of structural analysis focuses on the recognition and application of morphemes.

Morphemes are word parts such as base words, prefixes, inflections, and suffixes. Students can use structural analysis skills to find familiar morphemes within unfamiliar words, which helps them decode and determine the definitions of the new words. Identifying the word segments or morphemes also aids the proper pronunciation and spelling of new multisyllabic words.

Similarly, learning to use phonics skills with more difficult words depends on a reader's ability to notice syllable structures within words that have more than one syllable. **Syllabic analysis**, or **syllabication**, is a skill that students can use to analyze words and separate them into syllables.

Syllables are phonological units that contain a vowel sound. Teaching students how to break apart multisyllabic words into morphological and phonological units can keep them from being intimidated by long words, since these tools will help them identify syllable types, making longer words seem like a series of smaller words. The identified syllables can then be blended, pronounced, and/or written together as a single word. This helps students learn to decode and encode the longer words more accurately and efficiently with less anxiety. Thus, syllabic analysis leads to the rapid word recognition that is critical in reading fluency and comprehension.

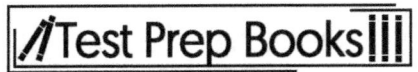

Phonics and Decoding

The following table identifies the six basic syllable patterns that should be explicitly taught during syllabic instruction:

Basic Syllable Patterns		
Name of Syllable Type	Characteristics of Syllable Type	Examples
Closed	A syllable with a single vowel closed in by a consonant.	lab, bog, an
Open	A syllable that ends with a single vowel. Note that the letter y acts as a vowel.	go, me, sly
Vowel-Consonant-Silent e	A syllable with a single vowel followed by a consonant then e.	like, rake, note, obese
Vowel Teams/Diphthongs	A syllable that has two consecutive vowels. Note that the letters w and y act as vowels.	meat, pertain, bay, toad, window
R-controlled	A syllable with one or two vowels followed by the letter r.	car, jar, fir, sir, collar, turmoil
Consonant le (-al, -el) Also called final stable	A syllable that has a consonant followed by the letters le, al, or el.	puddle, stable, uncle, bridal, pedal
Other final stable syllables	A syllable at the end of words can be taught as a recognizable unit such as cious, age, ture, tion, or sion.	pension, elation, puncture, stumpage, fictitious

Multisensory Approaches for Supporting Student Recognition of Nondecodable/Irregularly Spelled Words

While many words can be deciphered and spelled phonetically, that is, based on the sounds of their letters, non-decodable or irregular words cannot be read or spelled phonetically. Often, these words are taught as **"trick words"** or **"sight words"** to be recognized automatically as a whole word instead of as individual letter sounds. In the earliest grades, some sight words may be regular words that students can eventually decode with phonics (for example, it, can, not), and others are irregular words that cannot be easily decoded (for example, was, listen, though, once).

Traditionally, **non-decodable** or **irregular words** have been taught as whole words through visual memory and flashcards. However, not all students learn best this way. A **multisensory approach** provides alternative ways to learn by engaging other senses. Engaging different senses activates different parts of the brain, which makes content accessible for a greater variety of learners.

Writing, tracing, or building irregular words helps to increase recall, particularly if the student names the letters while writing or placing them in the correct order. **Rainbow writing**, or repeatedly tracing over the letters in a word with different colors of pencils or crayons, provides variety and fun. So does writing words with different types of letters (for example, bubble letters or fancy letters). Writing need not be limited to paper, though. Other options include writing on white boards or chalkboards, writing in sand or shaving cream, and writing in the air with a pointer finger. Alternatively, words can be built with letters on various media including paper letters, rubber stamps, letter tiles, magnetic letters, letters written on cubes or blocks, or letter beads. Letters can also be created using based modeling clay, or even posable wax sticks.

Flash cards provide a repetitive visual review of irregular words. They can also be used to create interactive games that further reinforce learning in a more kinesthetic and interactive way. The games bingo, Memory Match, and Go Fish are all easy to set up, explain, and play.

Worksheets can help to reinforce learning of irregular words. Teachers can create coloring sheets that have words in different sections; each word corresponds to a particular color, as in a color-by-number drawing. Read It, Write It, Build It worksheets display an irregular word with spaces in which the student can write the word and also build it with paper letters, rubber stamps, or other media. Students should also be given the opportunity to read and construct sentences containing the irregular words.

When repeating words and their spellings, using different sounds and gestures can make them memorable. For example, say "g-o, go" while pointing away from yourself, or spell "w-h-a-t" and then draw out the question "whaaaat?" while raising your arms in a questioning posture and tilting your head to the side. Chanting is another vocal and auditory way to reinforce words through repetition. There are also educational songs available online that reinforce the learning of particular sight words.

Finally, students may benefit from kinesthetically engaging with irregular words. Ask a student to jump to the card containing a particular sight word among those laid out on the floor. Alternatively, you can write the words on sticky notes and place them on the wall; have students jump to tap the appropriate word. You can also lay the cards on a table and have students swat them with a fly swatter.

Practice Quiz

1. All EXCEPT which of the following are considered non-decodable sight words?
   a. None
   b. Who
   c. Runner
   d. Said

2. Which of the following statements is true regarding decoding and encoding?
   a. Decoding is the spelling of words.
   b. Encoding helps students to recognize and read words quickly.
   c. Encoding is the application of letter-sound correspondences, letter patterns, and other phonics relationships.
   d. Decoding and encoding are learned in opposite stages or steps.

3. Which of the following displays a correct matching of an orthographic pattern with an example of that pattern?
   a. Consonant digraphs: player and jail
   b. Diphthongs: cow and pause
   c. Consonant Blends: foot and fool
   d. Schwa sound: harm and have

4. What is phonics?
   a. The study of syllabication
   b. The study of onsets and rimes
   c. The study of sound-letter relationships
   d. The study of graphemes

5. A teacher asks a student to identify which letter in the word "dog" makes the /d/ sound. The student points to the "d". What concept does the student understand?
   a. Decoding
   b. Encoding
   c. Phoneme-grapheme correspondence
   d. Affixes

See answers on the next page

Answer Explanations

1. C: The word runner is a decodable word because it follows the rules of phonics and is spelled phonetically. The other three choices are considered non-decodable sight words that students simply need to memorize because they are not spelled phonetically.

2. D: Choice *D* is correct because decoding and encoding are reciprocal phonological skills, meaning that the steps to each are opposite of one another. It is because of this reciprocal relationship that the development of phonics, vocabulary, and spelling are interrelated. The other answer choices are incorrect because they ascribe the wrong term to the given definition or skill.

3. B: The only correct example of an orthographic pattern is Choice *B*, diphthongs. Cow and pause both contain a diphthong ("ow" and "au").

4. C: When children begin to recognize and apply sound-letter relationships independently and accurately, they are demonstrating a growing mastery of phonics. Phonics is the most commonly used method for teaching people to read and write by associating sounds with their corresponding letters or groups of letters, using a language's alphabetic writing system. Syllabication refers to the ability to break down words into their individual syllables. The study of onsets and rimes strives to help students recognize and separate a word's beginning consonant or consonant-cluster sound, the onset, from the word's rime, the vowel and/or consonants that follow the onset. A grapheme is a letter or a group of letters in a language that represent a sound.

5. C: The student understands phoneme-grapheme correspondence because they are able to identify which letter corresponds with the /d/ sound.

Vocabulary and Fluency

Build, Expand, and Use Expressive and Receptive Vocabulary

Students have both an expressive and receptive vocabulary, meaning the words they use to talk (expressive) and the words that they understand (receptive). Both their expressive and receptive vocabularies need to be built and expanded upon to improve in their overall English skills. The best way to improve students' expressive and receptive vocabularies is by explicitly teaching new words, their definitions, and having students practice spelling and using those new words.

New vocabulary words should be chosen based on how relevant they are to what students are learning and reading at the time. When choosing which words to teach, it may be helpful to consider a word's tier. Tier one words are used commonly in speech and usually learned through oral language. Tier two words are used in many subjects, and tier three words are specific to particular subjects. Generally, vocabulary words taught through literacy falls within tier two.

To teach a new vocabulary word, start by saying the word and having students repeat it. Ask students to reflect on and discuss whether they're familiar with the word or its meaning. When possible, link the word with previously learned words or concepts.

Work with students and use appropriate resources (such as dictionaries) to help them develop a definition that plainly captures meaning in a way that is accessible to them. Use a vocabulary word in a sentence and ask students to do the same. Display vocabulary words, their definitions, and even related pictures on a word wall or in a graphic organizer.

Next, read aloud or have students read a level-appropriate text that includes the new vocabulary words. If reading aloud, stop to point out the vocabulary words as you read them. Walk through your thinking process of decoding the word and remind students of its meaning in this context. If students are reading independently, have them find and highlight new vocabulary words and review their definitions before they read the text.

Reinforce the learning of new vocabulary words with games like bingo, charades, and Pictionary. Challenge students to use the new words as much as they can when they're talking and writing and praise them when they do.

Teaching Vocabulary in Multiple Contexts

The key to embedding a vocabulary word in students' long-term memory is to expose them to the word multiple times in different contexts including various texts, images, audio, and multimedia. Teachers should use engaging and varied instruction to teach and reinforce new vocabulary words.

Maximize how often and in what ways students are exposed to vocabulary words by including definitions and examples as well as illustrations and anecdotes that make the words more memorable and meaningful for students. Gestures or miming can be used to physically engage students in the representation of a word.

In addition to having the teacher represent the word in auditory, visual, and kinesthetic ways, it is particularly beneficial to have students make their own personal connections to the word, thereby maximizing the likelihood that they will remember its meaning. Encouraging students to think-pair-share with a partner can help to stimulate thinking.

Other ways of encouraging students to make personal connections to words include using semantic maps to provide images, examples, synonyms, and even song lyrics or other attributes to help students categorize vocabulary words and connect them with prior knowledge. Alternatively, students can use sticky notes or pictures to add their visual or word-related (for example, synonyms, antonyms) impressions to a word wall.

It is important to vary the ways in which students practice their new vocabulary words. Flash cards with words on one side and definitions or related visuals on the reverse are helpful for students who learn through repetition. Alternatively, students can sort words into categories (for example, parts of speech; people, places, things; or categories of the students' choosing). Teachers can provide samples with vocabulary words used incorrectly and ask students to correct the mistakes. Finally, writing or speaking assignments in which students are tasked with correctly using new vocabulary words can also reinforce their learning.

Match an Instructional Method to Word Complexity

Texts should not be too hard or too easy for students. But how can teachers evaluate text complexity to ensure that they are giving their students appropriate materials? There are quantitative and qualitative methods of determining a text's level.

Quantitative measures attempt to objectively calculate the difficulty of a text. The most common quantitative measures are **readability formulas**, or mathematical equations that strive to calculate the difficulty of a text.

Fry's formula is a common readability formula that requires teachers to count the number of sentences and syllables in three random passages of one hundred words each. They then average each number and chart the two numbers on a Fry graph. The **Fry graph** uses the numbers to produce a suggested grade level for the text. While this method is a useful tool for estimating a text's complexity, teachers should take it with a grain of salt; Fry's formula does not account for variation within grade levels and the text's qualitative factors.

Vocabulary and Fluency

Fry Graph

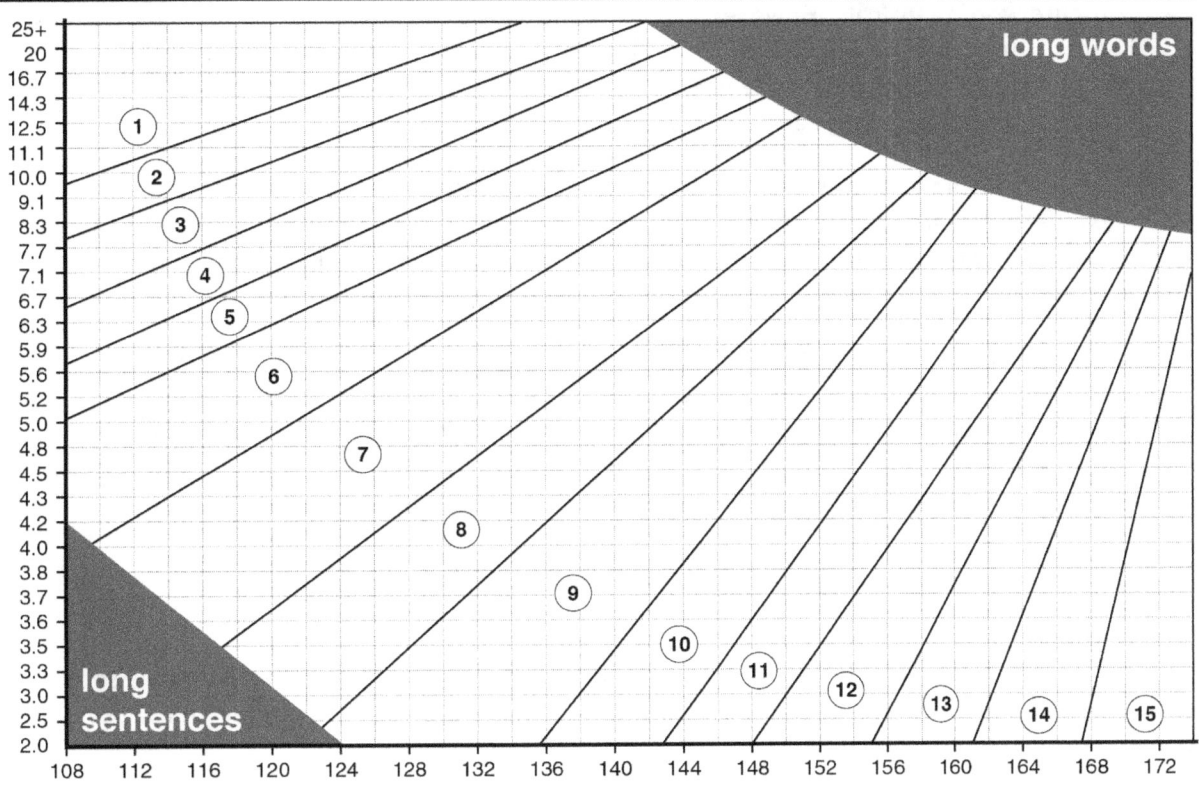

The other common quantitative measures are **Lexile text measures**. Like Fry's formula, these measures rate texts based on sentence length and word complexity. However, the Lexile method uses a database of text rankings instead of having teachers do the math themselves. It also gives texts a numerical rating from 0L to 2000L (L stands for Lexile) instead of a grade level. The most common way to test for a students' Lexile Reading Level is by having them take the Scholastic Reading Inventory, which sets the students' Lexile score level and identifies areas where the student excels and struggles in reading.

Another common way to determine student reading levels is through a Developmental Reading Assessment (DRA). The DRA is an individually administered standardized assessment of student reading skills. It generally consists of each student reading a teacher-selected passage or book, and then retelling the story to the instructor to assess for comprehension. While the student reads, the teacher should take notes of words that the student struggles with and any issues they have in accuracy, fluency, and prosody.

Qualitative measures identify subjective elements that affect the text's complexity. Below are some qualitative criteria that teachers can use to determine complexity.

- **Predictable structures** make texts easier to grasp, and they are especially useful in material intended for young children. For example, many fairy tales and children's books repeat questions and phrases. These predictable elements make the text less complicated, as children get into the pattern of the story and do not have to approach each repetition as an entirely new element.

- **Vocabulary** also determines a text's difficulty, and it cannot always be detected by quantitative measures. For example, the word "daft" consists of just one syllable, but it is clearly a more obscure word than "cat." However, Fry's formula would count the two words as the same level. Hence, teachers should skim the material to ensure the vocabulary is at an appropriate level. While texts should include some vocabulary words that will be new to students, an excess of new vocabulary renders reading so frustrating that students are likely to lose interest.

- Teachers should also consider the level of **background knowledge** required to understand a text. If easily learned background information is required (for example, basic historical context), teachers can present it to students before they begin to read a book. But if the background knowledge is complicated or far above the students' grade level, the book is not a good fit.

- Lastly, the **level of meaning** refers to how much abstract thought a text requires. Some texts only require students to understand the literal events of the book. More complex books, however, demand that students use abstract thought to make inferences and evaluate events. High levels of symbolism and abstract thought will be too difficult for younger students, while books that require only literal interpretation will likely seem boring to more mature students.

Teaching Word Solving

Context Clues

When using **contextual strategies**, students are introduced to new words indirectly within a sentence or paragraph. Contextual strategies require students to infer the meaning of a word by utilizing semantic and contextual clues.

Appositives and parenthetical elements can be very effective contextual strategies. **Appositives** are words that define or add meaning to a term that directly precedes them. An example of a sentence that includes apposition is: "Strawberries, heart-shaped and red berries, are delicious when eaten right off of the vine." In this sentence, the definition of strawberries ("heart shaped and red berries") directly follows the term and is introduced with and closes with a comma.

Parenthetical elements are specific types of appositives that add details to a term but not necessarily a definition. For example: "My cat, the sweetest in the whole world, didn't come home last night." In this sentence, the parenthetical element ("the sweetest in the whole world") further describes the cat but does not provide a definition of the word "cat."

Structural Analysis

Structural analysis skills are beneficial in the pronunciation of new words. When readers use **structural analysis**, they recognize affixes or roots as meaningful parts within a word. When a new word doesn't contain parts that are recognized by a student, the reader can use phonic letter–sound patterns to divide the word into syllables. The word parts can then be combined to yield the proper pronunciation.

Word maps are visual organizers that promote structural analysis skills for vocabulary development. They may require students to provide definitions, synonyms, antonyms, and pictures for given

Vocabulary and Fluency

vocabulary terms. Alternatively, **morphological maps** may be used to relate words that share a common morpheme.

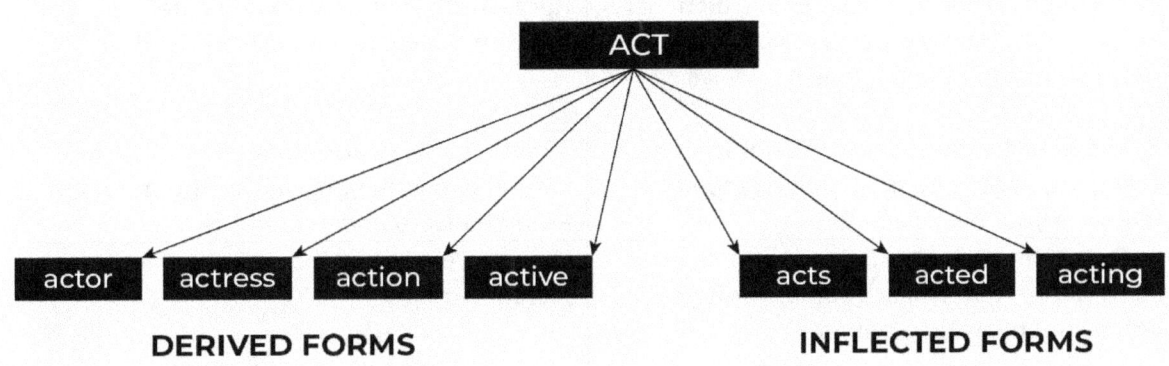

Similarly, **word webs** are used to compare and classify a list of words. Word webs show relationships between new words and a student's background knowledge. The main concept is in the center of the word web while secondary and tertiary terms stem off from it.

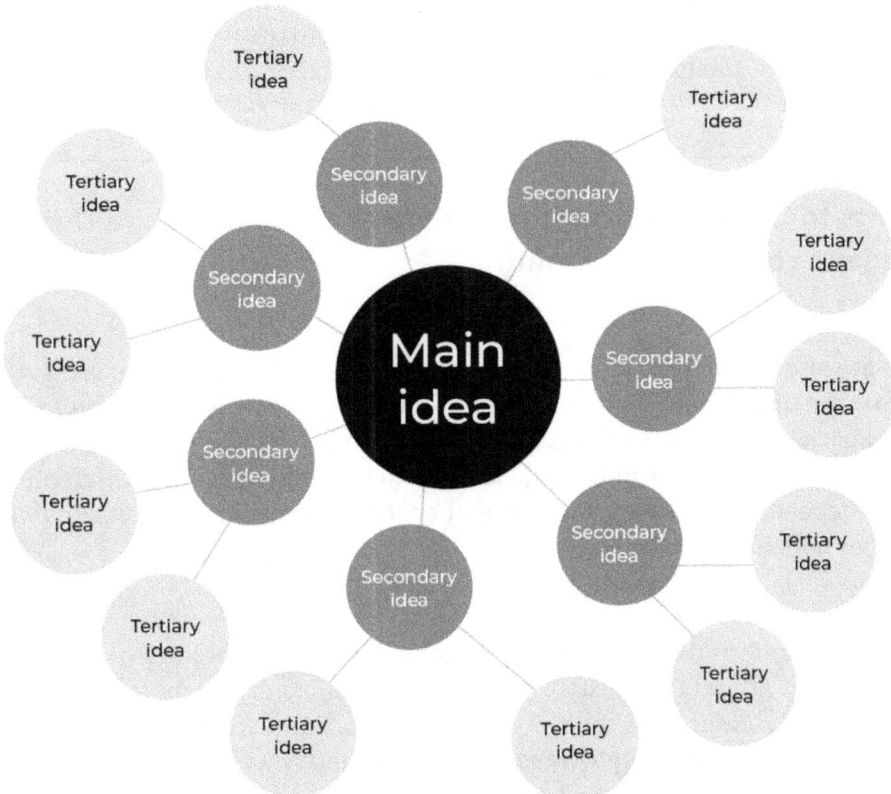

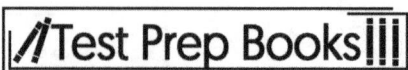

Vocabulary and Fluency

The table below identifies additional ways in which teachers can help students independently define unfamiliar words or words with multiple meanings:

Strategy	Examples
By Definition: Look up the word in a dictionary or thesaurus. Helps students realize that a single word can have multiple meanings.	Her favorite fruit to eat was a date. He went on a date with his girlfriend.
By Example: Invite students to offer their own examples, or to state their understanding following your own examples.	A myth is a story attempting to explain a natural phenomenon, such as the story of Prometheus to understand fire.
By Synonym: Understand that words have many different meanings. Some words are better synonyms than others.	She was very happy that day; her face was *radiant* with joy.
By Antonym: Teach student to look for words that have opposite meanings if the context of the sentence calls for its opposite.	Hannah was not happy that day; she was, in fact, very *depressed*.
By Apposition: **Apposition** is when the definition is given within the sentence.	The mango, a round, yellow, juicy fruit with an enormous seed in the middle, was ripe enough to eat.
By Origin: Identify Greek and Latin roots to figure out meanings of words.	In the word *hypertension*, the root "*hyper*" is a Greek word meaning "above" or "over."
By Context: Identifying what a word means by the surrounding text.	Water evaporates when it becomes hot, and the liquid turns into gas.

Guide Students to Understand a Wide Variety of Words through Direct Instruction and Independent Vocabulary Learning

Common

Common words are also called tier one words. They are the basic words that are used in everyday conversations that are often heard regularly. Most of the time, common words won't need to be taught through direct, explicit instruction. Students will usually have a basic knowledge of tier one words, and that knowledge can be built upon through regular use and spelling instruction. Students will grasp many common words independently through independent or shared reading, conversations with peers and family, and in other non-academic settings.

Contextual

Tier two words are also referred to as contextual vocabulary because they are more complex and can mean different things in different contexts. They are generally longer and more difficult to spell than common words, but not as difficult as content-specific words. Contextual words should be taught explicitly and directly and are best taught as spelling or vocabulary words. They're the types of words that are usually seen in academic settings, however they aren't specific to a certain field like content-specific words are. It's best to present contextual words to students in a variety of settings to help encourage understanding, memorization, and use.

Vocabulary and Fluency

Content-Specific

The top level of words that students will need to be taught are **content-specific,** or tier three, terms which students will need to commit to memory and understanding. They are words that apply to specific lessons, concepts, or ideas that are generally at a higher level. Some examples include *monarchy, isosceles,* and *quagmire.*

It is important as an instructor to use content-specific language when it's part of a lesson to build familiarity for the students hearing that language. However, tier three words don't need to be taught explicitly (as in vocabulary/spelling words) and should be covered naturally as the new concepts are learned. Students may also learn content-specific words independently through their own reading and studies.

Instructional Methods to Foster Students' Automaticity

Automatic Word Recognition, Accuracy, and Prosody for Reading Fluency

Word recognition is when students can recognize and read a word automatically and correctly. Phonics and sight word instruction help with accurate and automatic word recognition. Once students can readily identify and recognize words, then they can focus on the meaning of the text and development of reading comprehension skills.

Sight words, sometimes referred to as **high-frequency words**, are words that are used often but may not follow the regular principles of phonics. They are usually words that students can readily recognize and read without having to sound out. Students are encouraged to memorize words by sight so their reading fluency is not deterred through the frequent decoding of regularly occurring irregular words. In this way, sight word recognition aids reading fluency and reading comprehension.

Accuracy, Rate, and Prosody

Accuracy refers to the correct reading and pronunciation of words. **Reading rate** refers to the speed at which an individual reads within a given amount of time, often measured in words per minute. **Prosody** refers to the appropriate use of expression, intonation, emphasis, and tone when reading.

As word recognition increases, readers become less taxed with the interpretation of a text; thus, reading fluency and comprehension improve. When students read too quickly or too slowly for their skill level, they may lose reading comprehension. As accuracy and fluency increase, students begin to read aloud with appropriate prosody, and reading becomes a natural process.

Methods of Supporting Fluent Reading Behaviors at Multiple Levels

Phoneme Level

Phonemic awareness is the ability to understand the individual sounds (phonemes) that make up words. Being able to identify and manipulate phonemes is a foundational skill for those learning to read. Although phonemic awareness is auditory and does not directly involve reading, it is vital in establishing a strong connection to language.

By breaking words down into their smallest units, readers gain an essential understanding of how letters relate to sounds. Phonemic awareness is often used as a predictor for future success with reading. Once a student reaches the point of phonemic awareness, it is much easier to learn about phonics and the visual component of printed words. The student will be able to approach new words with the skills necessary to sound them out.

Vocabulary and Fluency

It is important for teachers to explicitly teach phonemes, one phoneme at a time. There are 44 phonemes, which are composed of the 26 letters of the alphabet. In many cases, phonemes have multiple different **graphemes** (or spellings). Without strong instruction, it is not uncommon for students to struggle with understanding basic word structure, phonics, and reading. Thus, the phoneme level is the initial base that is crucial in supporting fluent reading behaviors and setting students up for success.

Teachers can choose which phoneme to start with, but some good options include letters that make only one continuous sound which is included in the letter's name, like /s/, /m/, and /f/. Take care to not introduce letters that look or sound alike (e.g., d and b, /a/ and /u/).

Word Level

At the word level, instructors can focus on teaching word recognition and word identification. **Word recognition** is the ability to correctly and automatically recognize words at sight, without needing to use strategies. Word recognition is a prerequisite for fluent reading and reading comprehension. Practicing sight words is a great way to encourage automatic word recognition because it teaches the student to recognize the words at sight. While automatic word recognition can't necessarily be taught, it can be encouraged through regular interaction with print (e.g., independent and teacher-led reading/matching games/etc.

Word identification is the ability to recognize spoken or written words using letter patterns, context clues, knowledge of sight words, or other strategies. The best way to teach word identification is through thoroughly covering phoneme-grapheme correspondence, decoding strategies, and basic word structure.

To help with vocabulary, teachers might consider putting up a word wall with words relevant to the students' reading levels. This promotes word consciousness (an awareness of words) and provides visual reinforcement.

Passage Level

Reading aloud has been proven effective in strengthening reading fluency. Whisper-reading accompanied by teacher monitoring has also proven effective for students who do not yet display automaticity in their decoding skills.

Timed reading of sight phrases or stories also improves fluency with respect to rate. During a **timed reading** exercise, the number of words read in a given amount of time is recorded. Routinely administering timed readings and displaying the results in graphs and charts has been shown to increase student motivation.

Timed-repeated readings, where a student reads and re-reads familiar texts in a given amount of time, is a commonly used instructional strategy to increase reading speed, accuracy, and comprehension. Students read and re-read the passage until they reach their target rate.

Fluency, Vocabulary, and Comprehension

Fluency, vocabulary, and comprehension are necessary components of developing successful reading skills. They are the last three of the five essential components of reading instruction; the other two are phonemic awareness and phonics. All three component skills—fluency, vocabulary, and comprehension—are interrelated and rely on one another.

Vocabulary and Fluency

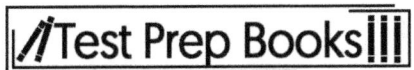

Fluency is the ability to read quickly and efficiently. Fluent reading can be compared to speaking in terms of speed and ease. **Vocabulary** refers to the knowledge of words, including their meaning and how they are used. **Comprehension** is the ability to understand what is being read. Understanding what we are reading is the ultimate goal when learning how to read.

These three skills are all connected. Without a strong understanding of vocabulary, it's difficult for a student to reach fluency. If a reader is pausing every sentence to look up a word or decode its meaning, that means that they are not reading smoothly or efficiently — the same goes for comprehension. Without knowing the meaning of the words, a student will struggle to understand the overall meaning of the writing. This could lead to misinterpreting the meaning and being unable to analyze texts.

Difficulty with reading also affects also other types of schoolwork. For example, a long-form question on a science test may be difficult to comprehend without a solid understanding of vocabulary. Likewise, without fluency, it will be difficult for a student to comprehend what they are reading. The correlation is so strong that reading fluency is often used as a predictor for later comprehension skills. Once fluency is developed, readers can tackle longer texts at a higher level. This expanded fluency leads to an expanded vocabulary as they learn new words.

There are many strategies to assist readers with learning these skills. To help with fluency, oral reading repetition may prove useful. This allows students to become comfortable with the text and practice reading aloud. Reading orally helps students connect reading to their speech, which improves the speed at which they read and the expression they give to the words.

One way to improve reading comprehension is to ask students to summarize what they have just read. This will help them think critically about the text and reread until they are sure that they understand. Instructors can also ask students to define certain words within the passage to help increase their vocabulary and improve their understanding of the entire passage.

Practice Quiz

1. Which of the following is NOT true of word walls?
   a. They promote strategic spelling, vocabulary development, common letter combinations, and common morphological units.
   b. They help students sort words they know, want to know, and have learned.
   c. They are useful during the phonetic stage of spelling development.
   d. They group words that share common consonant-vowel patterns or letter clusters.

2. What does a Developmental Reading Assessment mainly assess students for?
   a. Reading comprehension
   b. Reading speed
   c. Phoneme-grapheme correspondence
   d. Contextual strategies

3. Which of the following involves using the root word to understand the meaning of a larger word?
   a. Word maps
   b. Prosody
   c. Structural analysis
   d. Metacognition

4. What are the three interconnected indicators of reading fluency?
   a. Phonetics, word morphology, and listening comprehension
   b. Accuracy, rate, and prosody
   c. Syntax, semantics, and vocabulary
   d. Word exposure, phonetics, and decodable skills

5. Which of the following methods BEST supports fluent reading at the passage level?
   a. Timed reading exercises
   b. Word walls
   c. Phonemic awareness
   d. Sight word practice

See answers on the next page

Answer Explanations

1. B: Word walls are great tools for students as they learn to read, spell, and write. Because they help students pronounce unfamiliar words and provide visual contact with the word along with the auditory experience, they are particularly useful in the phonetic stage of spelling development. All the statements given are correct except Choice *B*, which describes KWL charts typically used for reading.

2. A: A DRA mainly assesses students' reading comprehension skills along with their accuracy, rate, and prosody.

3. C: Structural analysis is the concept of identifying the root words, base words, and affixes to help further understanding of larger words.

4. B: Key indicators of reading fluency include accuracy, rate, and prosody. Phonetics and decodable skills aid fluency. Syntax, semantics, word morphology, listening comprehension, and word exposure aid vocabulary development.

5. A: The best method for supporting fluent reading at the passage level is timed reading exercises. While all of the other answers help to improve students' general reading skills, timed reading exercises are best to encourage fluency.

Comprehension of Literary and Informational Text

Support Students' Listening Comprehension

Listening comprehension is an important aspect of learning and a skill that can be developed with time and effort. It can be enhanced by first activating students' background knowledge about the topic to be discussed; that way, they have some existing ideas to link the new information with. Having students preview a few questions about the topic before listening gives them guidance on what information to focus on. Pausing throughout a listening exercise to ask students questions or have them summarize what they've heard so far also promotes comprehension.

Students can practice listening comprehension through a variety of activities including conversing, following directions, and listening to stories. Teachers can help to build stamina in listening to stories by starting with reading shorter passages aloud and slowly increasing the amount students are expected to listen and absorb information.

Games are another great way to increase listening comprehension. The classic telephone game, in which each person takes a turn repeating to the next person what they heard from the previous person, is a great listening exercise. For another game, read a passage or story and then read it again with some changes to the details; have students identify the changes. In barrier games, two players sit on opposite sides of a visual barrier with identical materials in front of them. The players take turns describing how they are manipulating the materials, and the goal is to have identical setups at the end of the game.

Listening Comprehension in Relation to Reading Comprehension

Listening and reading are both learned, receptive language skills that use the same areas of the brain. They are interconnected with writing and speaking, which are productive language skills, so working on any one of these skills also improves the others.

Gough and Tunmer's "simple view" of reading breaks it into two parts: **decoding** (recognizing and sounding out words) and **language comprehension** (the ability to understand language and the meaning of the words read). Everyone first learns to comprehend language by listening, a necessary base skill for reading and reading comprehension. Therefore, students can better understand complex language and connections by listening first rather than by reading first. Exposing them to different vocabulary words through listening also provides a foundation for reading comprehension once they can decode words.

Early reading education focuses on decoding, but as students become more fluent decoders, the goal shifts to learning through reading: the ability to make sense of what is read.

Reading comprehension is notably affected by both students' vocabulary and background knowledge. Listening exercises can be used to develop language skills that are critical to reading comprehension. Language skills include the ability to:

- Recall literal descriptions, facts, and details
- Decipher the meaning of unknown words using context in the passage
- Connect text using inferences and prior knowledge
- Identify the main idea
- Summarize text

As younger students work to build their reading skills, non-print sources of information allow them to access technical language and topics better than they can through reading, and the non-print sources don't require them to expend mental energy decoding text. **Non-print sources** might include things like pictures or physical representations of associated words. The same is true of technical texts in older grades (for example, scientific writing). Therefore movies, performances, read-alouds, podcasts, and audiobooks are all good approaches to building listening comprehension, background knowledge, connections between existing and new knowledge, and vocabulary development that will strengthen students' reading comprehension. Students can also read along in a book or script while listening to an audio version, which enhances decoding and comprehension, particularly in struggling readers and English learners (ELs). All these auditory activities can be enhanced by asking students to make predictions and summarize information.

Another activity for bridging listening comprehension and reading comprehension is to have students act out a story they've listened to. The teacher can assign parts and provide scripts. Students work individually and in groups to increase their fluency and comprehension by practicing reading their parts, with support from peers, teachers, or parents, as necessary. After several days of practice, the whole class can perform the story together with scripts in hand.

Support Students' Speaking and Listening Skills as they Discuss Texts

Students learn best when they can share their thoughts on what they've read or written and receive feedback from their peers and instructors. For example, after reading a short story or poem, the teacher may ask a guiding question and have students discuss their answers with a partner. An effective method for this is think-pair-share, in which students *think* about a question the teacher poses about the text, then *pair* up with a partner or small group, and finally *share* their thoughts with their partner(s). It's important to circulate the room to monitor conversations, reminding students to give others time to speak before responding, thus reinforcing their speaking and listening skills.

It's important to explicitly teach the concept of active listening to students. Active listening means paying attention to the person who is speaking, understanding what they are saying, and reflecting on and remembering the information. Some techniques for improving students' active listening include directed drawings, games like telephone or Simon Says, and by modeling it for students by actively listening when they're speaking.

For writing, conferencing is frequently done in the revision stage. Conferences can be done in a one-on-one setting, typically between a student and instructor, or in a small group of students with guidance from the instructor. They are useful in that they provide an atmosphere of respect where a student can share their work and thoughts without fear of judgment. Conferences also allow the instructor to provide immediate feedback or prompt students for deeper explanations of their ideas. The most successful conferences have these characteristics:

- Have a set structure
- Focus on only a few points—too many are confusing or distracting
- Are solution based
- Allow students to both discuss their thoughts/works and receive/provide feedback for others
- Encourage the use of appropriate vocabulary
- Provide motivation and personal satisfaction or pleasure from reading and writing
- Allow a time where questions can be asked and immediately answered

Utilizing Background Knowledge

Background knowledge, or knowledge related to a text's topic, comes from readers' experiences as well as what they have learned by reading and listening. It allows readers to make connections that enhance their ability to read, summarize, decipher word meaning, and comprehend the text.

Using background knowledge makes it easier for students to make inferences about the meaning of a text by using their knowledge to build on the information explicitly provided in the text. It also helps readers interpret literary devices like metaphors and idioms, and it helps them interpret increasingly technical, subject-specific topics in informational texts.

A student's background knowledge, including the associations and categories of concepts in their mind, is also called their **schema**. Children who have greater exposure to life events have greater schemas. Thus, students who bring extensive background knowledge to the classroom are likely to experience easier automation when reading.

Readers' growth and development therefore critically rely on building background knowledge and activating it. Building background knowledge is not simply teaching students facts; instead, it involves strategically building interconnected webs of concepts that promote future learning. It's important for teachers to be aware of the diverse backgrounds of their students before they begin a text. This can help them identify areas of background knowledge that should be supplemented before reading.

One way to build and activate background knowledge across the curriculum is to give students time to read about and conduct in-depth research on a single topic using a variety of media. Teachers can pair fiction and nonfiction books on the same topic. Various media can be used to build and activate students' knowledge of different settings and cultures. Videos and virtual field trips can expose children to information that they will build on while reading a book set in an unfamiliar place or culture.

Activating students' background knowledge before they read a text helps them make connections to what they already know about a topic. One pre-reading strategy that works well with books that have many illustrations is a **picture walk**. Before reading, teachers draw students' attention to the cover, read the title aloud, and asking them to say what the story might be about. Flipping through the pages and stopping at illustrations, the teacher can ask questions about characters, plot, setting, and predictions (for example, "Who is this character?" "Where does the story take place?" "What do you think will happen next?") Picture walks activate background knowledge while also providing context that allows students to better decode vocabulary words.

Before and during reading, teachers can model behaviors that encourage students to make connections between what they are reading and their past experiences (text-to-self), other things they have read (text-to-text), and what they know about the world (text-to world). Students may share these connections verbally or through writing or drawing. While displaying the cover of a book, the teacher may say aloud, "This reminds me of the time I…" or "This book reminds me of the one we read….". By doing so, the teacher is modeling to students how to activate their background knowledge before reading a text.

Comprehension of Literary and Informational Text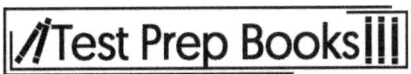

Methods for Teaching Comprehension

Reading comprehension involves the reader's use of prior knowledge, experience activation, prediction, text decoding, summarizing, and identification of the text's purpose to construct an understanding of the text's meaning.

Activating background knowledge before reading a new book can help students to recognize and decode new vocabulary words. Teachers may also ask students to predict what might happen in the reading based on the title, cover art, and illustrations (if there are illustrations). This is one of the first steps towards comprehension because it gets students thinking and developing an understanding of the overall meaning of the text.

Comprehension is best achieved through fluent reading. Phonics skills and decoding abilities both affect fluency, as does vocabulary knowledge. Students should be reading books at the appropriate level, or the level at which they can read at least 90 percent of the words. Harder texts disrupt the flow of their reading because the student will stop at unfamiliar words, which interferes with comprehension.

Having students slow down their reading speed also improves reading comprehension by giving them more time to process what they're reading. Reading aloud is one way to help students naturally slow down their reading speed. Further, rereading familiar texts facilitates decoding, enabling the student to read quickly and smoothly, which further increases comprehension.

Discussion, or verbal processing, of text before, during, and after reading helps students to remember what they've read and create meaning and connections that enhance comprehension. Ask guiding questions about what is happening in the book, what might happen next, and how the book relates to the students' experiences or other books they've read.

Similarly, teach students to pause and monitor their understanding of texts that they read independently, and teach them to reread sections that they don't understand. Using a journal or sticky notes, they can write down questions they have and words they don't understand. They can enhance understanding by defining vocabulary words they don't know and restating a passage in their own words, either independently or in a think-pair-share activity with a peer. They can also use what they've learned to predict what will happen next in the story and then read on to see if their prediction was accurate. Another way to reinforce understanding while reading is to ask students to create a mental picture of the story.

Graphic organizers are great tools to help enhance comprehension; they do this by organizing information and highlighting main ideas and relationships in a text. For example, **storyboards** show the order of events in a book, **flow charts** show cause-and-effect relationships among events in a story, and **Venn diagrams** compare and contrast. **KWL charts** (the acronym stands for *know, want, learn*) encourage the students to identify what they know about a topic (background knowledge), what they want to know about it, and what they've learned from reading a passage. Older students can be introduced to a variety of graphic organizers and then encouraged to use the type that works best for them.

After reading a story, students should be able to summarize it, discerning which information is important enough to include among the main ideas. Using **a five-finger retell activity** is an easy way to summarize; the five fingers are associated with five aspects of the text: characters, setting, plot, ending,

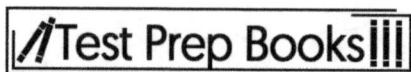

and favorite part. Another simple way to summarize is to have students identify what happened in the beginning, middle, and end of the text.

Comprehension questions (who, what, where, why, how) also help to gauge students' understanding after reading and assist them in making meaning of the text. Teachers can also have students write their own comprehension questions, which indicates whether they were able to accurately pull the main ideas from the text.

To accommodate students of various learning styles, teachers can vary the medium through which students exhibit their understanding of a text. Nontraditional media include comic strips, collages, skits, alternate endings, trivia, illustrated timelines, and oral presentations.

Using Metacognition for Comprehension and Analysis

Metacognition is an awareness of one's own thoughts and thinking process. This awareness can be especially useful during reading because it helps the student to constantly be considering *how* they are thinking about the text. A metacognitive learner is aware of their thinking process and can identify areas in which they need additional information or teaching.

When approaching reading instruction, teachers can encourage metacognitive thinking by guiding students to use phrases such as *I'm noticing*, *I'm thinking*, and *I'm wondering*.

Another strategy is to have students verbally respond as they read a passage. Students may quietly say, "hm" when they struggle to understand something, "oh" or "wow" when they learn something new, or "oops" if they realize they misunderstood something. Using verbal cues to keep students aware of their own thought processes is a great way to encourage metacognition.

A metacognitive reader needs to be able to ask themselves what they are reading about and what a passage is trying to say. Before reading a passage, the reader can enhance their ability to comprehend material by previewing the text for clues. This may mean making careful note of any titles, headings, graphics, notes, introductions, important summaries, and conclusions. The reader may make physical notes regarding these elements or highlight anything they think is important before reading. Often, a reader will be able to gain information just from these elements alone, but close reading is required to fill in the details.

In general, one of the best ways to encourage metacognition is through verbal cues. Reminding students verbalize what they are thinking and how they got to that conclusion helps them understand their own thinking processes. Ultimately, a student who is aware of their own thinking process is better equipped to recognize what they need to improve their comprehension.

Guiding Students' Self-Selection of Appropriate Texts

It's important as an instructor to give students the independence to self-select texts to encourage independent reading and comprehension. However, teachers can guide students in the self-selection process in a few different ways. First, it's important to set aside a time daily for self-selected, independent reading. In many schools, this is called DEAR (drop everything and read) time. It's also important to have a large classroom and school library that is stocked with books on multiple levels covering many different cultures and backgrounds.

Comprehension of Literary and Informational Text

To help students self-select books to read, the teacher can test for and provide them with an AR (Accelerated Reader) level (or an alternative reading program). The teacher can have students self-select books within their AR level to ensure that the difficulty of the text isn't too difficult or too simple.

Another method for self-selection is the five finger rule. With this method, students will select a book they want to read and turn to a random page and read it. While reading, they'll put up a finger for each word that they don't know. Once they finish the page, they'll see how many fingers they're holding up to judge the book's difficulty. If they have no fingers up, or just one, the book may be too easy. Two to three fingers is a good level of difficulty. Four or five fingers is too difficult for independent reading.

Differentiating Instruction, Tasks, and Materials for All Learners

Personalize Learning Experiences for Students of Different Needs

Differentiated instruction acknowledges that, while a group of students may be learning the same subject, the way each student learns and processes the subject is different. Differentiation involves looking at the different learning methods and reading areas and identifying which of them students respond to. Educators can then tailor, or differentiate, lessons to build on these skills and expedite the learning process.

There are three main areas in which teachers can differentiate instruction: content, process, and product.

The first method of differentiated instruction involves grouping students based on their ability levels and modifying the content to fit their different abilities. For example, the teacher can make assignments more challenging to engage higher level students and provide easier assignments to lower-level students. This helps keep learners engaged because higher level students won't lose interest due to lack of difficulty, and lower-level students won't become frustrated by assignments that are too difficult.

To find out a student's ability level in a certain skill, teachers can do informal or formal assessments. For example, to evaluate students' reading comprehension skills, the teacher may assign a formal reading assessment to the entire class that consists of reading a text selection and answering multiple choice questions about the passage. Afterward, the teacher will compare student assessment scores along with any other relevant data to group students based on their reading comprehension abilities.

Another way that teachers can modify instruction is through the process of instruction. This means giving students the option to learn in ways that work for them. For example, providing visual aids like posters and charts is a way of differentiating instruction for visual learners, who respond best to pictures and shapes rather than words. Kinesthetic learners do best when they're actively engaged in the learning process, which usually includes moving around, simulating relevant scenarios, or role play activities that allow for active learning (like reading and acting out parts in a play).

Finally, teachers can also modify the product during differentiated instruction, which includes offering students the choice in how they complete assessments. For example, a student may be able to submit their choice of an essay, a visual depiction or art project, a song, or a speech rather than simply having only one option. This allows learners to demonstrate their knowledge in a way that is engaging and inclusive to their learning style.

Choosing Materials that are Culturally Responsive to All Learners

In terms of materials, teachers should have texts in the classroom library that are bilingual and appropriate for English learners (ELs). Choose authors with various ethnic backgrounds rather than only including the most popular books. When possible, find authors who have similar cultures to the students in the classroom.

Students at different learning stages will require different materials. Teachers should have difficult books for advanced students and appropriate books for the students who still struggle with reading. Students will have greater motivation to read if they can easily understand and relate to the message of the text.

Use of Graphic and Semantic Organizers to Support Comprehension

Make Lessons Visual by Using Graphic Organizers

Visual aids are great tools that can help develop students' creativity and support their comprehension of text. **Graphic organizers** include webs, anchor charts, Venn diagrams, story boards, KWL charts, spider maps, and charts, all of which help students organize information and develop higher-level thinking.

Diagrams and graphic organizers provide students with visual clues to contrast and compare word meanings. From organizational charts and mind maps to Venn diagrams and more, visual aids help students readily see and analyze the similarities and differences in various word meanings.

Venn diagrams are a visual way of comparing two topics to find their similarities and differences. The student should list the two topics above each of the circles, and list details about each topic (differences) within its corresponding circle. Details that are true about both topics (similarities) should be listed in the middle.

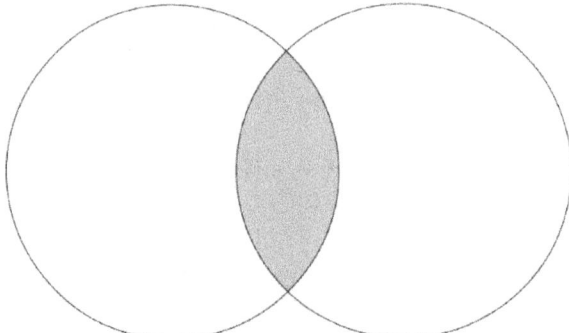

A KWL Chart includes three boxes, or sections, and is usually started before reading a passage or other texts. In the first box, the student will write what they know about a given topic or idea, and in the second box they will write what they want to know. Then, the class will together, or students will independently, read the text considering their preconceptions of the topic and thinking about what they wanted to know. Afterwards, the students will revisit the KWL chart for the last section, to add what

Comprehension of Literary and Informational Text

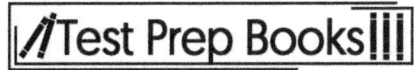

they learned from reading the text. At this time students should revisit their K and W sections to note whether what they knew was true, and whether or not they learned what they wanted to know.

K-W-L Chart

What I **K**now	What I **W**ant to know	What I **L**earned

There are many different types of charts, but the most common type are T-charts, which consist of two columns. T-charts are usually used to categorize two different ideas or concepts and highlight the differences or the relationship between the two. For example, students can use a T-chart to categorize

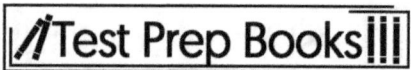
Comprehension of Literary and Informational Text

the cause-and-effect relationships in a piece of text. In one column, the student can write the cause of something and then add the corresponding effect in the second column.

T- CHART

TOPIC:	TOPIC:

Semantic Organizers
To strengthen reading comprehension, educators should consider the introduction to word webs and **semantic organizers**. Semantic organizers are maps of words that visually depict the meaning and

relationship between words, phrases, and concepts. They can be as complex as the example below, or as simple as writing the word in the center of a paper and drawing lines to all of its synonyms and related phrases.

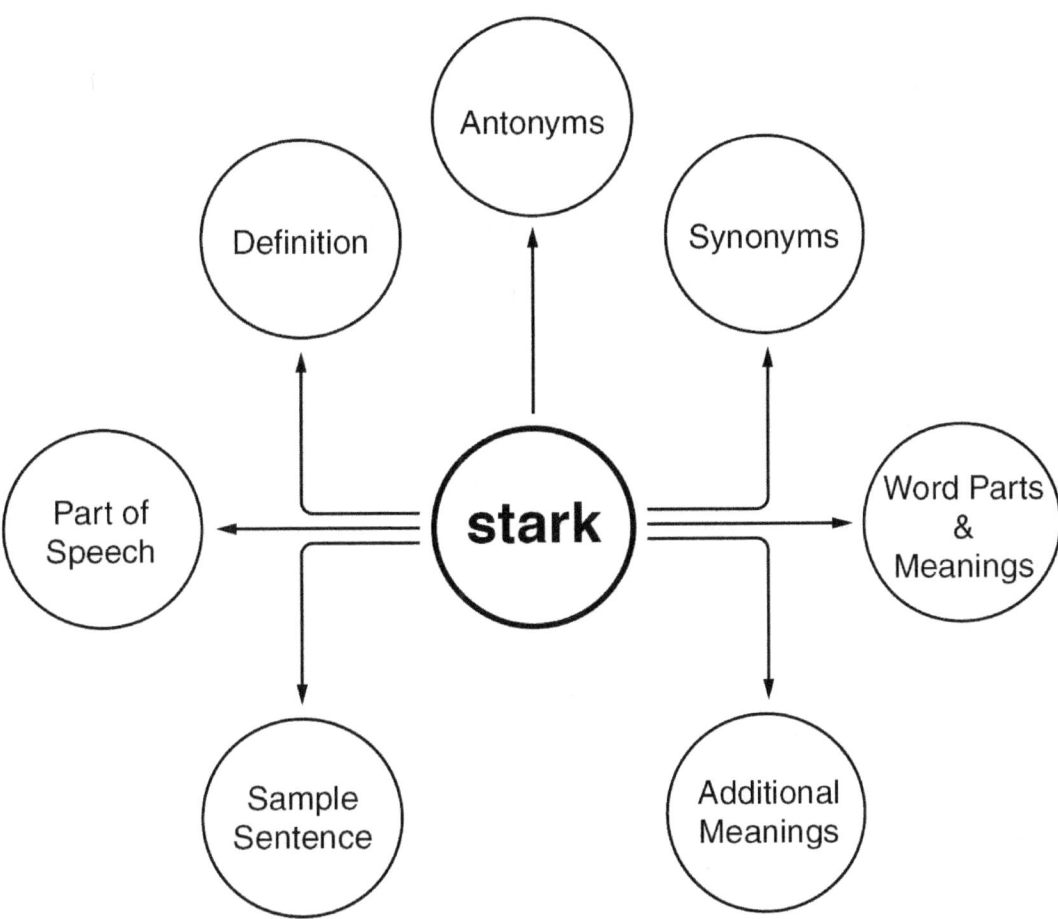

Genres, Structures, and Features of Literary Texts

A **genre** is a category of literature that possesses similarities in style and in characteristics. Based on form and structure, there are four basic genres:

Poetry
Poetry is fiction in verse that has a unique focus on the rhythm of language and focuses on intensity of feeling. It is not an entire story, though it may tell one; it is compact in form and in function.

Prose
Prose consists of fictional works written in standard form with a natural flow of speech and without poetic structure. Fictional prose primarily utilizes grammatically complete sentences and a paragraph structure to convey its message.

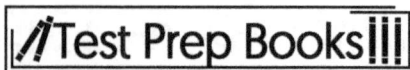

Comprehension of Literary and Informational Text

Drama
Drama is fiction that is written to be performed in a variety of media, intended to be performed for an audience, and structured for that purpose. It might be composed using poetry or prose, often straddling the elements of both in what actors are expected to present. Action and dialogue are the tools used in drama to tell the story. **Comedy** is any drama designed to be funny or lighthearted. **Tragedy** is any drama designed to be serious or sad.

Literary Nonfiction
Literary nonfiction is prose writing that is based on current or past real events and/or people. It includes straightforward accounts as well as those that offer opinions on facts or factual events. Nonfiction has the following subgenres:

- **Informational Text:** This is text written to impart information to the reader. It may have literary elements such as charts, graphs, indexes, glossaries, or bibliographies.

- **Persuasive Text:** This is text that is meant to sway the reader to have a particular opinion or take a particular action.

- **Biographies and Autobiographies:** These texts that tells intimate details of someone's life. If an author writes the text about someone else, it is a **biography**. If the author writes it about himself or herself, it is an **autobiography.**

- **Communicative Text:** This is text used to communicate with another person. It includes such texts as emails, formal and informal letters, and social media posts. This content often consists of two-sided dialogue between people.

Story Elements
There are five key elements to every story: characters, setting, plot, conflict, and resolution. Each story must have these elements to flow smoothly and maintain its structure. The characters of a story are who the story is about, the setting is where it takes place, the plot is the events that take place, the conflict is the major problem that needs to be solved often at the climax of the story, and the resolution is way that the conflict is resolved. Each of these concepts should be explained explicitly and in detail, and teachers should have students practice identified each of the five story elements in every text that they read.

Characters
Characters are the story's figures that assume primary, secondary, or minor roles. **Central or major characters** who are those integral to the story—the plot cannot be resolved without them. A central character can be a **protagonist** or hero. There may be more than one protagonist, and they don't always have to possess good characteristics. A character can also be an **antagonist**—the force against a protagonist.

Character development is when the author takes the time to create dynamic characters that add uniqueness and depth to the story. **Dynamic characters** are characters that change over the course of the plot's timeline. *Stock* characters are those that appear across genres and embrace stereotypes—e.g., the cowboy of the Wild West or the blonde bombshell in a detective novel. A **flat character** is one that does not present a lot of complexity or depth, while a *rounded* character does. Sometimes, the **narrator** of a story or the **speaker** in a poem can be a character—e.g., Nick Carraway in F. Scott Fitzgerald's *The Great Gatsby* or the speaker in Robert Browning's "My Last Duchess." The narrator might also function as a character in prose, though not be part of the story—e.g., Charles Dickens's narrator of *A Christmas Carol*.

Setting
The **setting** is the time, place, or set of surroundings in which the story occurs. It includes time or time span, place(s), climates, geography—man-made or natural—, or cultural environments Emily Dickinson's poem "Because I could not stop for Death" has a simple setting—the narrator's symbolic ride with Death through town towards the local graveyard. Conversely, Leo Tolstoy's *War and Peace* encompasses numerous settings within settings in the areas affected by the Napoleonic Wars, spanning from 1805 to 1812.

Plot, Conflict, and Resolution
The **plot** is what happens in the story. Plots may be singular, containing one problem, or they may be very complex, with many sub-plots. All plots have an exposition, a conflict, a climax, and a resolution. The **conflict** drives the plot and is something that the reader expects to be resolved. The plot carries those events along until there is a **resolution** to the conflict.

Point of View
The **point of view** is the position the narrator takes when telling the story in prose. If a narrator is incorporated in a drama, the point of view may vary; in poetry, point of view refers to the position the speaker in a poem takes.

First Person
The **first-person point of view** is when the writer uses the word *I* in the text. Poetry often uses first person, e.g., William Wordsworth's "I Wandered Lonely as a Cloud." Two examples of prose written in first person are Suzanne Collins's *The Hunger Games* and Anthony Burgess's *A Clockwork Orange*.

Second Person
The **second person point of view** is when the writer uses the pronoun *you*. It is not widely used in prose fiction, but as a technique, it has been used by writers such as William Faulkner in *Absalom, Absalom!* and Albert Camus in *The Fall*. It is more common in poetry—e.g., Pablo Neruda's "If You Forget Me."

Third Person
Third person point of view is when the writer utilizes pronouns such as him, her, or them. It may be the most utilized point of view in prose as it provides flexibility to an author and is the one with which readers are most familiar. There are two main types of third person used in fiction. **Third person omniscient** uses a narrator that is all-knowing, relating the story by conveying and interpreting thoughts/feelings of all characters. In **third person limited**, the narrator relates the story through the perspective of one character's thoughts/feelings, usually the main character.

Tone
The **tone** of a story reflects the author's attitude and opinion about the subject matter of the story or text. Tone can be expressed through word choice, imagery, figurative language, syntax, and other details. The emotion or mood the reader experiences relates back to the tone of the story. Some examples of possible tones are humorous, somber, sentimental, and ironic.

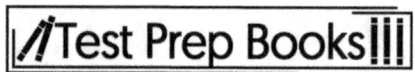

Comprehension of Literary and Informational Text

Literary Devices

Figurative Language

Figurative language uses words in ways that are different than their original meaning, often using devices such as simile, metaphor, hyperbole, personification, or allusion to enhance one's writing. **Creative writing** tends to employ more non-literal expressions than academic or informative writing. Educators should give students ample time to experiment with different kinds of figurative language, especially when switching from creative to more academic writing.

Figurative language can be used to give additional insight into the theme or message of a text by moving beyond the usual and literal meaning of words and phrases. It can also be used to appeal to the senses of readers and create a more in-depth story. This is often seen in more descriptive writing.

It is also considered a rhetorical device in that figurative language is used to play on the *meanings* of words as well as the *sounds* of words. These kind of literary devices are more likely found in poetry but may also be found in non-fiction writing like speeches.

Figurative language, including metaphor, simile, hyperbole, personification, allusion, puns, onomatopoeia, oxymoron, idiom, litotes, alliteration, and synecdoche should all be taught through direct instruction and explained in great detail. Students should be well-versed in identifying each example of figurative language and note how they differ from one another. Another way to encourage understanding of figurative language is to read books that contain plenty of figurative language, and to identify where it's used throughout the text.

Nuance of Words

Nuances are the small differences that words can have in meaning depending on their context, often referred to as "shades of meaning". For example, although "lovely" and "good" mean nearly the same thing literally, they have two very different nuances. A reader will picture a "lovely chair" much differently than a "good chair" despite having the same definition.

This is because words can convey different levels of intensity or emotion despite meaning the exact same thing. Nuance can be taught with plenty of examples of words that mean the same thing but have two different nuances (like "lovely" and "good", "cheerful" and "elated", or "small" and "petite").

Alliteration

Alliteration refers to the repetition of the first sound of each word. Alliteration can be used to build emotion in a piece, to cause the reader to slow down, or to add rhythm and structure to a piece. Recall Robert Burns' opening line:

> My love is like a red, red rose

This line includes two instances of alliteration: "love" and "like" (repeated *L* sound), as well as "red" and "rose" (repeated *R* sound). Next, assonance refers to the repetition of vowel sounds and can occur anywhere within a word (not just the opening sound). Here is the opening of a poem by John Keats:

> When I have fears that I may cease to be
>
> Before my pen has glean'd my teeming brain

Comprehension of Literary and Informational Text

One great way to teach alliteration to students is through tongue twisters like "Peter Piper picked a peck of pickled peppers". Most students enjoy getting the chance to try and repeat tongue twisters, making them a fun and memorable activity. Engaging in different types of instruction will help students form deeper mental connections to what alliteration is. Another way to teach alliteration is through poetry and song lyrics. Using engaging material, teachers should have students identify the examples of alliteration they can find within popular lyrics or poetry.

Strategies for Supporting Readers as they Construct Literal and Inferential Meaning

Literal Comprehension
Literal comprehension refers to the reader's ability to understand the actual meaning of texts. This is not meant to be complicated. It means literally understanding the facts, setting, plot, etc. of what is being read.

To bolster literal comprehension, show students how to ask pertinent questions. When they are reading stories, children should learn to ask who the characters are, what happened, where the story is taking place, and in what order the events occurred. Teachers can use graphic organizers like KWL charts and Venn diagrams to have students identify things they learned in the story. Teachers can also check for literal comprehension by conducting an assessment after reading with questions from the text.

Inferential Comprehension
Inferential comprehension requires students to understand the hidden context or unstated meaning of a text. They should be able to explain why an action occurred and what they think will happen next. This also referred to as "making inferences", when a student reads a selection of text and is able to understand a further meaning that isn't directly stated.

When it comes to inferential comprehension, children need to recall the facts that occurred in the story and what those facts represent. They should ask the following questions:

- Why did this happen?
- How might the characters feel?
- What might happen next?
- How important is "X" character?

Teachers can encourage students' inferential comprehension by modeling it while reading, making inferences aloud, and pointing out when students make inferences while reading. It's also important that the concept of making inferences is taught within direct instruction, and teachers should ask guiding questions to help students make inferences throughout the text, like those listed above.

Author's Use of Language
Author's use of language is the particular way that authors write, including the words, phrases, and sentence structure they use and how it works to convey the author's meaning. Whether an author chooses to use more literal or figurative language is an example of their use of language. The way that an author uses language directly impacts the tone and flow of story. One way to explain author's use of language to students is by providing them with two paragraphs that tell the exact same story. In one paragraph, the language should be literal and direct, simply telling what happened. In the other paragraph, the story should include figurative language and elements like similes and metaphors. After

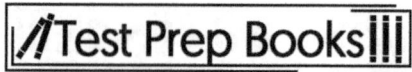

reading, the teacher should discuss with students how the author's use of language makes the two stories different.

Types, Structures, and Features of Informational Texts

Informational text provides readers with factual information and is designed to lead the reader to a central idea or conclusion. It is important that students understand the different types, structures, and features of informational text.

Informational Text Types

- **Literary Nonfiction:** The most common type of informational text is literary nonfiction. It's also called creative nonfiction because the true story or event is told in an engaging, short story style. The reader may feel like they are reading a story, but all of the details are based on facts rather than fiction.

- **Expository:** Expository texts are most often used to provide detailed information about a person, thing, place, or event. This style of writing is most often seen in news articles and is usually presented in a literal, direct tone.

- **Argumentative:** Argumentative, or persuasive, texts generally present a problem or idea and work to convince the reader of a certain belief.

- **Procedural**: This kind of writing is called "how-to" writing, and it is typically in the context of a product. A list of instructions, features, or ingredients may be included in this type of text.

To teach the informational text types, teachers should present examples of each kind and have students read them and identify which type the text falls under.

Informational Text Structures

The following organizational structures are most common:

- **Problem/solution**—organized by an analysis/overview of a problem, followed by potential solution(s)

- **Cause/effect**—organized by the effects resulting from a cause or the cause(s) of a particular effect

- **Spatial order**—organized by points that suggest location or direction—e.g., top to bottom, right to left, outside to inside

- **Chronological/sequence order**—organized by points presented to indicate a passage of time or through purposeful steps/stages

- **Comparison/Contrast**—organized by points that indicate similarities and/or differences between two things or concepts

- **Order of importance**—organized by priority of points, often most significant to least significant or vice versa

Comprehension of Literary and Informational Text

The first step in identifying a text's structure is to determine the thesis or main idea. A **thesis statement** indicates the writer's purpose and may include the scope and direction of the text. It is usually presented at the beginning or end of a text, and it may be explicit or implicit.

Once a reader has a grasp of the thesis or main idea of the text, they can better determine its organizational structure. Test takers are advised to read informational text passages more than once in order to comprehend the material fully. It is also helpful to examine any text features present in the text including the table of contents, index, glossary, headings, footnotes, and visuals. The analysis of these features and the information presented within them, can offer additional clues about the central idea and structure of a text. The following questions should be asked when considering structure:

- How does the author assemble the parts to make an effective whole argument?
- Is the passage linear in nature and if so, what is the timeline or thread of logic?
- What is the presented order of events, facts, or arguments? Are these effective in contributing to the author's thesis?
- How can the passage be divided into sections? How are they related to each other and to the main idea or thesis?
- What key terms are used to indicate the organization?

Next, test takers should skim the passage, noting the first line or two of each body paragraph—the *topic sentences*—and the conclusion. Key **transitional terms**, such as *on the other hand*, *also*, *because*, *however*, *therefore*, *most importantly*, and *first*, within the text can also signal organizational structure. Based on these clues, readers should then be able to identify what type of organizational structure is being used.

Teachers can promote understanding of text structure by having students practice identifying the structure of each text they read. A good way to do this is by starting simple with paragraphs, and the teacher can provide a paragraph that exemplifies each type of text structure (cause/effect, comparison/contrast, spatial order, chronological order, problem/solution, and order of importance). After reading each paragraphs, students should match the paragraph to its' text structure.

Features of Informational Text
Nearly every type of informational text contains features that make the text easier to navigate and comprehend. For example, the title, subtitles, headings, and subheadings help readers understand what the following passages and text will be about.

Informational text features like table of contents, indexes, and glossaries can make navigation of the text easier and help readers find information faster. They can make it easier to find a certain chapter or concept that the student needs to know.

Text features like italics and bold print, help draw attention to certain words and phrases. They're often used to provide definitions or add emphasis to a certain word.

Visual features like diagrams, charts, graphs, and pictures help further comprehension through visual means. They add additional meaning and information to the text in another way.

Using Technology to Support Students

Critically Examine Online Resources and Foster Digital Literacy

In order to have an education conducive to college and career readiness and success, students need online research and digital media writing skills.

With current digital technology, the writing process has become a much more collaborative experience. In higher education and in career settings, collaborative skills are essential. Publishing and presenting are now simplified such that completed work is often read by a wide variety of audiences. Writing can be instantly shared with parents, peers, educators, and the general public, including experts in the field. Students are more apt to take an interest in the writing process when they know that others are reading their writing. Feedback is also simplified because so many platforms allow comments from readers. Teachers can be interactive with the students throughout the process, allowing formative assessment and integration of personalized instruction.

Reference Materials and Media Resources

It is critical that educators teach students how to locate credible information and to reliably cite their sources using bibliographies. Platforms and apps for online learning are varied and plentiful. Here are some ideas for how to use technology for writing instruction in the classroom:

- Use a projector with a tablet to display notes and classwork for the group to see. This increases instructional time because notes are already available rather than having to be written in real-time. This also provides the ability to save, email, and post classwork and notes for students and parents to access on their own time. A student can work at their own pace and still keep up with instruction. Student screens can be displayed for peer-led teaching and sharing of class work.

- More technology in class means less paperwork. Digital drop-boxes can be used for students to turn in assignments. Teachers can save paper, keep track of student revisions of work, and give feedback electronically.

- Digital media can be used to differentiate instruction for multiple learning styles and multiple skill levels. Instead of using standardized textbook learning for everyone, teachers can create and collect resources for individualizing course content.

- Digital textbooks and e-readers can replace hardback versions of text that are prone to damage and loss. Students can instantly access definitions for new words, as well as annotate and highlight useful information without ruining a hardbound book.

- Library databases can be used to locate reliable research information and resources. There are digital tools for tracking citation information, allowing annotations for internet content, and for storing internet content.

- Mobile devices may be used in the classroom to encourage reading and writing when students use them to interact with classmates in digital spaces like Google Classroom.

- PowerPoint and other presentation software can be used to model writing for students and to provide a platform for presenting their work.

Comprehension of Literary and Informational Text

- Web quests can be used to help guide students on research projects. They can get relevant information on specific topics and decide what pieces to include in their writing.

- Students can write about technology as a topic. They can "teach" someone how to use various forms of technology, specific learning platforms, or apps.

- Students can learn to create webpages, usually through a central class website that offers the ability for each student to create an individual page on the site.

- Online feedback and grading systems can be used. There are many to choose from and the school district will often select one system like Gradebook or Skyward to use for every school, teacher, and classroom. Online grading systems allow parents, students, and teachers to view student grades in real time.

- Game show-style reviews can be created for units of study to use on computers or on an overhead projector.

- Students can make or use pre-created online flashcards to study concepts and prepare for tests.

- Publishing tools can be used to publish student work on the web or in class newspapers or social media sites.

Support Active Learning Across Content Areas
Using Technology Tools for Effective Communication

Different technological tools serve different functions. To function in the developing world, students need to learn and understand **digital literacy**—the knowledge, dexterity, and critical thinking skills involved in using technology to create, evaluate, and present information. The best techniques for instructing students on choosing and using technological tools involve educating them on the advantages and disadvantages of each, demonstrating how to use them, breaking down their different aspects, assigning students homework or projects in which they will utilize different technological resources, and instructing them on when it is appropriate to use each kind. The most common types of tools used for communication are as follows:

- Smartphones/apps
- Email
- Microsoft Office
- iMovie
- Skype
- Twitter
- Facebook
- Instagram
- Google Drive
- Various blogging websites
- Online bulletin boards
- Wikis

A good way to introduce students to varying technological tools is by using them in the classroom. It would be helpful to teach students how to use a PowerPoint presentation, for example, by giving a PowerPoint presentation. If a student asks a question to which the teacher does not know the answer,

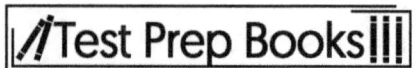

Comprehension of Literary and Informational Text

they can discover the answer together by using a reliable source on the Internet, projecting the process on the board, so that they can see exactly how it's done. Students can also receive homework and updates on school and classroom events through a personal blog or class bulletin board the teacher has designed so that they may become familiar with using online communication. Students can also be assigned to use personal blogs to practice and improve their writing skills.

The most effective method for learning new skills is a hands-on approach. Students can be educated on the pros and cons of each technological tool, but the best way for them to learn is to allow them to find out for themselves by assigning projects and asking them to give the reasoning behind choosing a specific tool. For example, they may be asked to do a project on some aspect of the Revolutionary War by choosing a media format. Ideas may include the following:

- Doing a presentation
- Filming and editing a video re-enactment of a great battle
- Writing a script in Microsoft Word or in a Google doc and having classmates act it out
- Creating Facebook statuses from the viewpoints of the forefathers in modern colloquial language
- Having a "Twitter war" between the British and the Colonials
- Asking various people to participate in a collaborative Wiki or Google Doc in which many people give their versions of aspects of the Revolutionary War
- Writing a blog narrating life as a soldier
- Posting photos of the signing of the Declaration of Independence

Students can then give their presentations to the classroom so that students can learn about the topic through different presentation styles.

Another way to engage students in using technology is to have them communicate with each other through the various methods of communication—e.g., starting a class Google Doc, creating a classroom Facebook group, or using a discussion board. This is also an excellent opportunity to encourage students to use Standard English through all methods of communication to enhance their writing skills and instill a sense of professionalism, which they will need throughout their lives.

For example, requiring that all students use complete sentences, proper spelling, and grammar through Facebook, Twitter, or blogs associated with homework or projects will encourage them to do so in their daily lives as well. Another example is requiring that students select tweets from their favorite celebrities or politicians, analyze their meaning and purpose, correct their grammar and spelling, and re-tweet them in the correct way. There are countless ways in which technology can be used in the classroom to enhance students' understanding of digital communication; all it requires is a little creativity.

Evaluating Technology-Based Strategies

It is hard to find a technological tool that will not be useful for students to explore. The more a student engages with the numerous different types of technology, the more digitally literate that student will

Comprehension of Literary and Informational Text

become. Each type is effective and brings value to the table in its own way. When evaluating the effectiveness of a specific technology-based strategy, it's important to consider how this method is enhancing the student's digital literacy, as well as their critical thinking and communication skills. It is also necessary to evaluate the technology itself by asking relevant questions:

- Is it appropriate for the average age of the students in the classroom?
- Is it user friendly?
- Does it work consistently?
- Are there multiple ways to get help on learning how to use it?
- Are there trouble-shooting options?
- Does it have good reviews?
- Is it relevant to the content of the curriculum?
- Does it support and align to the learning objective?
- Is it more distracting than it is useful?
- Is it a tool that is/will be used often in the real world?
- Can it be used for more than one project or assignment?

One very effective teaching strategy is **collaborative learning**, in which two or more students work together to develop a project, work through an idea, or solve a problem. This method allows for students to play off each other's strengths and different experiences and learn how to communicate with their classmates to achieve goals. Technology can be used for collaborative learning in Google Drive, Skype, Google Hangouts, Nearpod, Padlet, and Periscope, in creating PowerPoint presentations together, or by conducting surveys with websites like Survey Monkey.

Another effective teaching method is **discussion**, in which students are given a topic or create a topic themselves and then use technology to engage in discourse. This can be done via discussion boards, such as ProBoards or Boardhost, or done live through programs such as Skype or Hangouts. Discussion strategies are extremely effective for enhancing communication skills and digital literacy.

A third method is **active learning**, in which the student engages in activities such as reading, writing, or teaching the subject to another student. Blogging is a great way to encourage active learning as it provides a medium through which students can reflect on what they've learned and respond to comments posted by the teacher or other students. Most of the suggestions made in the previous section—making presentations, creating video re-enactments, writing scripts, having mock Twitter or Facebook comment wars—are all forms of active learning. These types of activities solidify events, ideas, and skills in a student's mind in a way that memorization or flashcards do not as they utilize many different types of thinking and interaction.

One method that a teacher may employ depending on the class and circumstances is **distance learning**. Distance learning is any type of teaching method in which the student and teacher are not in the same place simultaneously. Many professors utilize distance learning through different kinds of technologies, including a live virtual lecture, computer simulations, interactive discussions, and virtual/audio learning environments. These strategies have their advantages in that one teacher can teach a large number of students and multiple locations, and students can communicate with fellow classmates across the globe.

Auditory learning is a strategy in which a student learns through listening. This typically happens via recorded lectures that can be downloaded as podcasts onto a classroom website, discussion board, or some other audio-simulated learning environment. **Visual learning** is learning through watching, in which ideas and concepts are illustrated through images, videos, or by observing a teacher complete a task, explain a concept, or solve a problem. This can be achieved through recorded videos, cartoons, virtual lectures, or by sitting in the classroom. Additionally, **kinesthetic learning** is active learning through physical interaction with an object or actively solving a problem, as opposed to passively listening or watching.

Every student has a different learning style which is unique to them—some learn better through listening while others learn better through doing. The best teaching methods employ all different learning strategies so that all the senses are engaged and every student has a chance at learning material based on their individual learning needs. Technology offers educators the tools do that.

Practice Quiz

1. Students are reading a text that explains the origins of a popular candy company, beginning with the founder's birth to the present-day status of the company. Which type of text structure does this text likely follow?
    a. Cause/effect
    b. Comparison/contrast
    c. Chronological order
    d. Order of importance

2. Why is annotation a beneficial exercise for students?
    a. It teaches them to think independently.
    b. It helps them learn to identify key points.
    c. It teaches them to write faster.
    d. It helps shy students engage in discussion.

3. Which of the following are transitional terms?
    a. Maybe; kind of
    b. Like; when
    c. Because; also
    d. Soon; above

4. A class silently reads a passage on the American Revolution. Once they are done, the teacher asks the students to name the two sides who were fighting, the reason they were fighting, and the winner. What skill is the teacher gauging?
    a. Orthographic development
    b. Fluency
    c. Comprehension
    d. Phonics

5. A teacher assigns a writing prompt in order to assess her students' reading skills. Which of the following can be said about this form of reading assessment?
    a. It is the most beneficial way to assess reading comprehension.
    b. It is invalid because a student's ability to read and write are unrelated.
    c. It is erroneous since the strength of a student's reading and writing vocabulary may differ.
    d. It is the worst way to assess reading comprehension.

See answers on the next page

Answer Explanations

1. C: The text is in chronological order because it follows the timeline of the company from the very beginning to the present day.

2. B: Annotating texts teaches students to determine what information is important. Choices *A* and *C* may be true in some cases, but they are not necessarily related to annotation. Choice *D* is false because annotating does not involve class discussion.

3. C: The words "because" and "also" are transitional terms because they help transition sentences from one idea to another.

4. C: Comprehension is the level of content understanding that a student demonstrates after reading. Orthographic development is a cumulative process for learning to read, with each skill building on the previously mastered skill. Fluency is an automatic recognition and accurate interpretation of text. Phonics is the ability to apply letter-sound relationships and letter patterns in order to accurately pronounce written words.

5. C: A student's reading ability will most likely differ when assessed via a reading assessment versus a writing sample. There are five types of vocabulary: listening, speaking, written, sight, and meaning. Most often, listening vocabulary contains the greatest number of words. This is usually followed by speaking vocabulary, sight reading vocabulary, meaning vocabulary, and written vocabulary. Formal written language usually utilizes a richer vocabulary than everyday oral language. Thus, students show differing strengths in reading vocabulary and writing vocabulary.

Written Expression

Writing as a Recursive Process that Supports Self-Evaluation and Expression

Like with any complicated processes, writing development begins with the simplest form of indiscernible scribbles and progresses to fully formed words and, finally, to clearly written sentences and paragraphs. This is a complicated cognitive process that takes time and instruction to improve.

With very young students, emphasis can focus on simply making letters clear. After all, letters and word formation are the starting blocks of written language. The next phase in development can focus on actually creating words and making sure they are spelled correctly. When students are at the sentence development stage, grammar and linguistic rules become a priority. The foundations of the English language need to be firm for students to have good writing. When students have progressed to more advanced levels and are composing fully formed sentences with a specific purpose, it's time to incorporate content-related feedback.

Feedback at all levels of writing development is crucial; this is how students will learn to correct mistakes and strengthen growing skills. Instructor feedback must be clear while also being sensitive to the students' struggles or backgrounds. Differentiated instruction may be required to bolster students' writing skills. Feedback on the initial writing, or first draft, is key. The instructor should be able to assess any difficulties and then steer the student toward improving their writing in the revision stage. After revisions, instructors should examine how effective their feedback was in helping the writing improve overall.

Written expression refers to the ability of the writer to fluidly communicate meaning and purpose throughout the composition. Essentially, this refers not only to how clear the central focus of the piece is but how well the ideas surrounding the central focus are presented. If the writer can't successfully express the meaning and implications of the idea, the writing will not be strong.

Effective written expression utilizes detailed, clear communication. A writer doesn't need to unload elaborate diction throughout the paragraphs. Such an embellishment can be distracting to the reader, which actually defeats the principles behind effective writing. Sentences should be direct and emphasize language that, while engaging, remains simple enough for the audience to understand. This doesn't mean abstaining from using advanced words but rather keeping sentences direct and to the point. Students should avoid rambling line after line. Avoiding exaggerating language or overdramatic phrasing is also important. Not only can this confuse the reader, but it can also harm the writer's credibility.

A simple formula for effective writing is to introduce an idea, discuss it, and then make a conclusion. This applies for the written piece as a whole but must also be used within individual paragraphs. If a writer just introduces idea after idea with no substance, the reader is left with unsubstantiated claims. Without supporting evidence to understand the view, the reader is left with only opinion. With the implementation of facts and supporting details, this opinion is strengthened. Thus, the reasoning behind the central idea is clearly executed and can be considered seriously. This helps the writer achieve credibility.

Paragraph coherence is vital for effective written expression. Paragraph sequencing and information placement are essential to streamlining the entire piece. Evidence and supporting information should be used to transition from one section to another, up to the conclusion. This enables the information to be clearly expressed. The author should strive to write in a way that, as the piece progresses, the focus becomes clearer and more convincing. By the conclusion of the written piece, the author should also restate their thesis to solidify their views and reasoning.

Systematic, Explicit Methods to Teach the Steps of the Writing Process

An introduction to the writing process might begin with a discussion. Teachers can gauge students' knowledge about writing by asking them questions about the writing process, its steps, and its purpose. They may also ask about students' previous experiences with writing. It's important to emphasize that writing is a process, not something students complete once and move on from.

Before expecting students to write, teachers should model each step in the writing process. Based on a chosen topic, the teacher can brainstorm aloud, walking through their thought process and describing different methods for recording the results (for example, in a list, in an outline, or on a concept map). Students would then be given time to brainstorm about their own topics.

Next, the teacher may choose to share samples of drafts from previous students or ones they've completed themselves. Even better, they can model their thought process aloud in front of the class, writing a rough draft while the students watch.

Teachers can display **anchor charts** to remind students what to include (for example, beginning, middle, and end, and details) and what not to worry about in this step (for example, mistakes, neatness, structure).

The **revision step** includes changes like removing unnecessary information, adding helpful information, and moving text to improve flow. The teacher can point out the issues in the rough draft and make the appropriate edits, incorporating the use of a checklist or anchor chart if one is provided.

In the editing process, the teacher reviews the spelling, grammar, and punctuation of the students' writing. The **editing step** is a great time to catch any errors the students may have missed. This is a good time for a teacher-student conference to review the draft. Peer conferences are also an option. The teacher can act out a peer review conference with one student to show students what is expected from a peer review conference.

Before final submission, the teacher should share the final versions of the papers they've been working on as models, highlighting their strengths in how they meet the parameters of the assignment, especially compared to the rough drafts. Before publishing their final polished draft, students should read over their writing aloud and add necessary details (for example, a title and illustrations). Again, a checklist or anchor chart can be helpful.

Once all writing is complete, students can take turns sharing the final product in small groups or with the class. Peer feedback at this point can help guide future improvements in the next writing assignment.

The easiest way to guide the writing process is to give students time to work on it in class. This allows the teacher to check on students' progress and offer feedback as they go through the writing process. To promote improvement, teachers can make each part of the writing process (for example, rough draft, peer review conference) a part of the final grade for the assignment.

Strategies for Integrating Reading and Writing

Summarizing

Teaching students to summarize is another comprehension and analysis technique. They can complete rewriting exercises here as well. Students just need to do three things when they employ this technique. They should recall what they read, identify the main point of the texts, and exclude unnecessary information. Summarizing does not have to take place after students have finished reading texts; they can do it as they go along. Eventually, this type of summarizing will be second nature, and students will be able to assess the texts without stopping.

Teach students to summarize information. For example, you could ask students to take notes on the most important points in a text and then write a summary. Younger students do better with simple oral summaries, while older students can handle more complicated written work. Summarizing is a great way to improve comprehension. It also tests analysis skills, as students need to discern which points are important and which are just details.

Annotation

Teach your students to annotate texts by highlighting and making notes in the margins. For example, you might have students read a confusing passage, then annotate it by highlighting the most important pieces of information and defining difficult words. By annotating texts, students learn to recognize central points and research words or background information that they do not understand.

Teach your students to take notes. For students who are just learning to take notes, it may be helpful to practice reading a text as a class and making notes on the board. Teach your students useful skills like summarizing, picking out main points, and outlining arguments. For example, you could read a passage aloud and ask all the students to take notes. You could then have the class compare notes and write a collaborative summary of the text.

Have students apply metacognition to their comprehension by identifying the elements of a text that they cannot understand. For example, if a student says, "I don't understand this book," ask them to think about the specific aspects that confuse them and build a more detailed phrase like "I don't understand what happens in chapter four," or "I can't understand this word."

Digital Tools

Digital tools are an invaluable resource for the classroom. They can enhance the learning experience by providing new forms of engagement. This benefits both students and teachers. Apps, videos, websites, and games are just a few examples of digital tools that can provide unique educational content. These tools can help students work on collaboration and creativity. Digital tools can also improve accessibility in the classroom. Educational videos can aid visual learners, audiobooks can provide auditory learners with a new reading experience, and kinesthetic learners may learn new skills from building games. These are just a few examples of how digital tools may benefit different types of students.

When implementing digital tools, student engagement often sees great improvement. Maintaining student interest is a major key to effective learning. Teachers also benefit from digital tools in the learning space. They can record lectures for at-home learning, ease workloads by automating repetitive tasks such as grading, and streamline communication with students and their families. Overall, both students and teachers may benefit from the implementation of digital tools in the classroom. Technology is always advancing, and it is wise to take advantage of the benefits it offers.

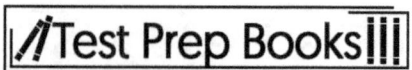

Communication

One of the most important elements of a successful classroom is communication. There are plenty of digital tools that can foster and encourage communication and help create an environment where students feel welcome and ready to learn. Websites like ClassDojo allow for instant and effective communication between teachers, students, and parents. It allows for a digital classroom points system, where teachers can click a button to give a student a point. Students can also take quizzes, participate in whole class online discussions, and keep track of their progress on their ClassDojo account.

Another great communication tool is Google Classroom. It's a comprehensive digital classroom where students can communicate with teachers instantly, view lessons and materials, and complete and submit assignments and assessments.

Remind is another communication tool that is commonly used in the classroom. It allows parents and students to sign up for classroom messages. Through Remind, the teacher can put out whole-class reminders and messages, message individual students or parents, and track assignments and upcoming tests.

The Seesaw app and website is also great for promoting communication between teachers, parents, and students. It allows for collaborative learning and showing off student work. It's a great way to encourage students to their best in hopes of having their work featured on Seesaw.

Writing

One of the fundamental parts of learning to write well is having your work reviewed. There are many online platforms where students can practice their writing skills and submit it for feedback. This includes both fiction and non-fiction writing. Hemingway Editor is a free website and app that will point out common errors in writing: spelling, grammar, run-on sentences, and confusing wording.

If a student is interested in getting feedback from other writers, Scribophile is an online workshop where students can submit their work for critique. This is useful for writers of all skill levels.

At the classroom level, resources like Microsoft Word and Google Drive make it easy for students to create, edit, and store their writing. They also spelling and grammar checks along with other writing tools that students can access as they revise their work.

Collaboration

There is a plethora of online platforms that encourage collaboration in the classroom. They allow students to share what they are learning with one another, work on group projects, and communicate virtually. Some platforms are utilitarian; others are designed for fun. A utilitarian option is Google Drive, which allows students to share documents, presentations, and more. A fun option is Kahoot, which students can use to create quiz games that an entire class can participate in. This kind of collaborative creation is one way to get students to practice their teamwork.

Publishing

In terms of publishing, students should use resources like Turnitin, Scribbr, and Grammarly to check for plagiarism or any major issues. While Turnitin only looks for plagiarism, other websites like Grammarly check for the overall tone, flow, and textual features (like grammar, spelling, etc).

Written Expression

Characteristics and Appropriate Instructional Methods for Teaching the Various Types of Writing

It is important to use appropriate instructional methods for teaching the various types of writing. Although general writing tips can be helpful, different writing types require different instructional methods. The types of writing include expository, persuasive, narrative, and descriptive.

Expository writing is meant to inform the reader about a concept. In this case, you would want to teach about the use of evidence in writing. Persuasive writing is meant to convince the reader of an argument. In this case, you could want to teach about how to present an opinion in writing. Narrative writing tells a story. In this case, you would want to teach about characters and plot. Descriptive writing presents the setting; it can also present imagery. In this case, you would want to teach about how to engage readers with metaphors and similes. These are just a few examples of how writing types differ and how instruction should vary accordingly.

Informational/Expository

Expository or **informational writing** presents facts and information. Academic essays are one example of this type of writing. Due to its logical purpose, expository writing should be clear and linear. Writers should use strong evidence to back up their claims. Sources used should be scholarly and unbiased. However, just because expository writing is factual, it does not have to be boring. It is important to keep the writing engaging to capture readers' interest.

A proven way to teach informational and expository writing is by having students practice writing about a subject they choose. First, students should research and choose 2-3 sources about a subject they like. The teacher can set parameters on what categories students can choose from (animals, historical events, etc), provide a list of topics to choose from, or allow complete freedom of choice. After selections have been made and sources verified, the student should begin on the writing process, and the teacher may offer formative feedback as the student writes. At the time of writing, the teacher should display anchor charts on the format of informational essays (the first paragraph should be an introduction, followed by one or more body paragraphs, and finally a concluding paragraph).

Argument/Persuasive/Opinion

Persuasive writing is used to convince readers of a particular opinion; writing should be informative and evidence based. However, unlike expository writing, it also aims to sway readers to believe in a particular position.

One example of persuasive writing would be an article on climate change that also presents a solution that the writer wants readers to support. This type of writing should have a strong thesis statement that lets readers know what the main idea is. It may also be important that the writing read as if it were speaking directly to the reader. This is one effective way to draw the reader in to what the author is saying. Students can practice persuasive writing by responding to a situation or question posed by the teacher. To encourage student participation, the teacher could make the assignment fun by asking students to write a persuasive essay on the next sport the class should play or next book the class should read.

Narrative

The goal of **narrative writing** is to tell a story, whether fictional or not. An example of fictional narrative writing would be a novel; autobiography is nonfictional narrative writing. Narrative writing is often the most personal and creative form of writing. There are multiple types of narrative writing, such as linear, non-linear, viewpoint, and descriptive. Narrative writing may include characters, plot, and setting. These elements help the writer to make the story imaginative and unique. Although narrative writing comes with a high degree of writer freedom, effective narrative writing requires just as much skill and practice as the other types of writing.

One way to have students practice narrative writing is to have them write an essay detailing the events of their summer or winter break. Display anchor charts reminding students of the necessary aspects of narrative writing (characters, plot, setting) and provide plenty of resources for independent spelling and grammar help (dictionaries, thesauruses, digital resources).

For fictional narrative writing, be sure to do a brief review on the structure of a story. First, the beginning sets the stage for the action, it's followed by a conflict or problem, then a sequence of events follow the initial conflict that bring rising tension or drama, the tension reaches a height at the climax of the story where readers should be "on the edge of their seats", and finally is followed by falling actions or events that happen after the climax that lead into the resolution and the ending of the story. Further enhance students' knowledge of stories by reading class novels and short stories regularly.

Spelling and Grammar

Methods to Connect the Teaching of Decoding and Encoding as Reciprocal Skills

Teaching of decoding and encoding should begin with linking sounds to letters and eventually combinations of letters. To decode a word, students must attribute sounds to letters and blend them together. To spell a word, they must break the word they've heard into individual sounds, remember the letter(s) and patterns that make those sounds, and write them down, which is much more challenging. Simultaneous explicit and systematic instruction in decoding and encoding positively affects students' abilities to read, write, and spell.

Teacher-led practice involves the teacher clearly articulating a sound (phoneme) before having students say the sound and then write the letter(s) that correspond with the sound. Once these skills have been solidified, students can begin segmenting the words they hear, identifying the phonemes, and writing the letter(s) that represent them. First, teachers teach explicitly through modeling, and then they walk students through active, guided practice before having students practice independently. Make practice engaging and multimodal (for example, by incorporating hand gestures and manipulable items).

Instruction should be systematic, starting with simple information and using lessons that sequentially build upon one another toward increasingly complex ideas. The curriculum should outline the progression of teaching letter combination patterns (phonemic awareness) and how they are used in reading and spelling rules. This incremental approach promotes mastery in one topic or skill before moving on to new topics and skills.

Written Expression

Approaches to Spelling Development

Spelling development systematically occurs in stages. Through each of these stages, multisensory strategies can be explicitly taught to help enhance a child's spelling development. Here are the spelling development stages as well as different strategies to help development in each of those stages:

Pre-phonetic stage: This stage begins an individual's spelling development, inclusive of key indicators such an incomplete understanding of the alphabetic principle and letter-sound correspondences. Students in this stage participate in **precommunicative writing**, characterized by the jumbling of abstract letter forms rather than a cohesive group of recognizable letters. These writing samples can be used as informal assessments to monitor students' understanding of the alphabetic principle and of letter-sound correspondences.

Pre-phonetic stage of spelling development

Semi phonetic stage: In this stage, students have an understanding that letters denote specific sounds. Though this understanding is there, the student may continue to struggle with letter recognition. In the students' writing, they may use individual letters in place of entire words (e.g., U for *you*). In other instances, they may omit multiple syllables within a word altogether. Writing in this stage is likely still incomprehensible. To aid in understanding the students' work, teachers can ask students to include drawings to supplement their writing samples.

Semiphonetic stage of writing

Phonetic stage: At this point, students will have mastered letter-sound correspondences and can spell most VC and CVC words. Although their physical representation of letters may be incorrect, phonetic spellers can write each letter of the alphabet. Due to their limited sight vocabulary, their spelling may be incorrect; however, these incorrectly spelled words are likely still phonetically accurate. Additionally, students are likely to use one letter to represent a digraph or letter blend (e.g., *f* for /ph/). Spelling instruction of common consonant patterns, short vowel sounds, and common affixes or rimes can begin during the phonetic stage. Word walls are beneficial during this stage as they provide visual groupings of words that share common consonant-vowel patterns or letter clusters. Students should be encouraged to contribute words to the wall. As a result, word walls promote strategic spelling, vocabulary development, common letter combinations, and common morphological units.

Phonetic stage of writing

Transitional stage: In this stage, the student is growing in their sight vocabulary and has a sustainable understanding of letter-sound correspondences. As a result, their spelling dependence on phonology decreases and instead, their dependence on visual representation and word structure increases. The student should be able to spell most conventionally spelled words but may still struggle with many irregular words. During this stage, instructors should differentiate spelling instruction. It is necessary that instruction be guided by data collected through informal observations and assessments so that lessons can be personalized, especially in the areas of sight word recognition, morphology, etymology, reading, and writing.

In this stage, students are also ready to begin learning about **homophones**; these are words that sound the same but have different spellings and meanings (e.g., *their* and *there*). Additionally, students should begin writing full sentences. Writing reinforces phonics, vocabulary, and correct spelling of words.

Transitional stage of spelling

Conventional/Correct stage: By this stage, students are comfortable with the basic rules of phonics and spell most words correctly. They can work with consonants, multiple vowel-consonant blends, homophones, digraphs, and irregular spellings. They should be able to recognize incorrectly spelled words. It is at the conventional stage that spelling instruction can begin to focus on content-specific vocabulary words and words with unusual spellings. Students should practice this content-specific language across a variety of activities and subjects when relevant. Students can keep track of words that they consistently spell incorrectly or find confusing in word banks so they can isolate and eventually eliminate their individualized errors.

Teaching the Structure of Written Language

Rules of Grammar and Mechanics

Before educators teach reading or writing, they should themselves be masters of the language. They should know the conventions of grammar, punctuation, spelling, and structure of language to communicate clearly. They must also be able to interpret what students are saying to either affirm or revise it. Teachers are responsible for differentiating instruction so that students at all levels and aptitudes can succeed with language learning. Teachers need to be able to isolate gaps in skill sets and decide which skills need intervention in the classroom.

Written Expression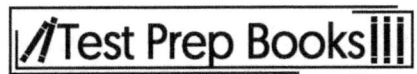

Syntax

Syntax is the way that words are ordered within a sentence and how the sentence flows grammatically. Syntax defines the grammatical rules necessary for sentence flow, like the fact that sentences need at least a subject and a verb.

A basic rule of syntax is that sentences usually follow the subject-verb-object order. For example, look at the sentence "Sally ate breakfast." Sally is the subject, ate is the verb, and breakfast is the object. The only way that this sentence makes sense is in the subject-verb-object order. Rewriting it like "Sally breakfast ate", or "Breakfast Sally ate", would make it not flow correctly or make sense.

Teachers need to have mastery of the conventions of English including:

- Nouns
- Collective Nouns
- Compound Subjects
- Pronouns
- Subjects, Objects, and Compounds
- Pronoun/Noun Agreement
- Indefinite Pronouns
- Choosing Pronouns
- Adjectives
- Compound Adjectives
- Verbs
- Infinitives
- Verb Tenses
- Participles
- Subject/Verb Agreement
- Active/Passive Voice
- Adverbs
- Double Negatives
- Comparisons
- Double Comparisons
- Prepositions
- Prepositional Phrases
- Conjunctions
- Interjections
- Articles
- Types of sentences
- Subjects and Predicates
- Clauses and Phrases
- Pronoun Reference Problems
- Misplaced Modifiers
- Dangling Participial Phrases
- Punctuation
- Periods
- Commas
- Semicolons and Colons
- Parentheses and Dashes
- Quotation Marks
- Apostrophes
- Hyphens
- Question Marks
- Exclamation Points
- Capitalization
- Spelling
- Noun Plurals
- Prefixes and Suffixes
- Spelling Hurdles
- Abbreviations
- Pronunciation
- Homonyms and other easy mix-ups

When teaching structure, grammar, and mechanics, it's important for teachers to remember a few key things. First, all the conventions of English (as listed above) should be taught explicitly through direct instruction. Teachers should not expect students to stumble upon the concepts through reading or other means.

One fun way to encourage student engagement is by turning the grammar skill or mechanic that students are learning about for the week into a scavenger hunt. For example, after a lesson on quotation marks, the teacher may have students bring written or photographic evidence of where they spot quotation marks in their daily activities. It's important to engage students in lessons in a variety of ways to increase their understanding and memorization of the concepts.

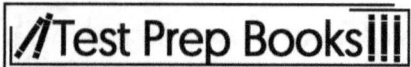

When it comes to writing, it's important to continually review and edit student work to display proper mechanics and grammar. For example, if a student continually begins sentences with a lowercase letter, it's important to correct their work with a capital letter instead and have a conversation with the student about the mechanic of capitalization and its use at the beginning of every sentence.

Practice Test

1. In the word *shut,* the *sh* is an example of what?
   a. Consonant digraph
   b. Sound segmentation
   c. Vowel team
   d. Rime

2. When students identify the phonemes in spoken words, they are practicing which of the following?
   a. Sound blending
   b. Substitution
   c. Rhyming
   d. Segmentation

3. What is the alphabetic principle?
   a. The understanding that letters represent sounds in words
   b. The ability to combine letters to correctly spell words
   c. The proper use of punctuation within writing
   d. The memorization of all the letters in the alphabet

4. Print awareness includes all EXCEPT which of the following concepts?
   a. The differentiation of uppercase and lowercase letters
   b. The identification of word boundaries
   c. The proper tracking of words
   d. The spelling of sight words

5. Sharon is a first-grade teacher who assigned her students a rhyming project to come up with three words that rhyme with "cat". One of her students returned the project with the words "dog", "hi", and "to". The teacher realizes that the student is struggling with which of the following skills:
   a. Phonological awareness
   b. Phoneme deletion
   c. Phoneme blending
   d. Directionality

6. Structural analysis would be the most appropriate strategy in determining the meaning of which of the following words?
   a. Extra
   b. Improbable
   c. Likely
   d. Wonder

7. A student spells *eagle* as *EGL*. This student is performing at which stage of spelling?
   a. Conventional
   b. Phonetic
   c. Semi phonetic
   d. Transitional

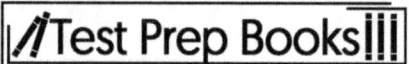

8. The teacher writes the letters "s" "t" "a" "k" and "e" on the board and asks students to chorus the word, to which they correctly answer "stake". Then, the teacher asks the students to chorus "stake" again, but without the /s/ sound, but many students have trouble and mispronounce the new word. The teacher notes that the class is struggling with which of the following concepts?
   a. Phoneme substitution
   b. Phoneme deletion
   c. Phoneme-grapheme correspondence
   d. Blending

9. Ms. Brown has just finished a lesson introducing the lowercase letter "b" to her students. Which of the following is the best letter to introduce in her next lesson?
   a. Lowercase "d"
   b. Lowercase "v"
   c. Lowercase "p"
   d. Lowercase "s"

10. A student can follow the directions "sit down, get out a pencil and two pieces of paper". However, when asked a question, she doesn't respond. Which type of language skills does the student have?
    a. Expressive
    b. Basic
    c. Receptive
    d. Auditory

11. Which of the following is the most appropriate assessment of spelling for students who are performing at the pre-phonetic stage?
    a. Sight word drills
    b. Phonemic awareness tests
    c. Writing samples
    d. Concepts about print (CAP) test

12. Phonological awareness is best assessed through which of the following?
    a. Identification of rimes or onsets within words
    b. Identification of letter-sound correspondences
    c. Comprehension of an audio book
    d. Writing samples

13. The identification of morphemes within words occurs during the instruction of what?
    a. Structural analysis
    b. Syllabic analysis
    c. Phonics
    d. The alphabetic principle

14. A child who is given the word "bat" and then sounds out the phonemes /b/ /a/ /t/ understands which of the following concepts?
    a. Blending
    b. Segmenting
    c. Manipulation of syllables
    d. Substitution

Practice Test

15. Nursery rhymes are used in kindergarten to develop what?
    a. Print awareness
    b. Phoneme recognition
    c. Syllabication
    d. Structural analysis

16. High-frequency words such as *be, the*, and *or* are taught during the instruction of what?
    a. Phonics skills
    b. Sight word recognition
    c. Vocabulary development
    d. Structural analysis

17. What is a helpful way to encourage expressive language development at the early intermediate literacy stage?
    a. Fill in the blank activities
    b. Silent reading
    c. Word web activities
    d. Partner-shared reading

18. Samantha is in second grade and struggles with fluency. Which of the following strategies is likely to be most effective in improving Samantha's reading fluency?
    a. The teacher should encourage Samantha to stop and sound out the words she is unfamiliar with while reading.
    b. The teacher should have Samantha read multiple grade-level passages one time each.
    c. The teacher should review the different types of genres with Samantha before she begins reading.
    d. The teacher should have Samantha read one grade-level passage multiple times.

19. Which is the largest contributor to the development of students' written vocabulary?
    a. Independent reading
    b. Directed reading
    c. Direct teaching
    d. Modeling

20. The study of roots, suffixes, and prefixes is called what?
    a. Listening comprehension
    b. Word consciousness
    c. Word morphology
    d. Textual analysis

21. Which graphic organizer would be best for listing cause-and-effect relationships within a piece of text?
    a. Venn diagram
    b. T-chart
    c. KWL chart
    d. Spider map

22. The teacher introduces a new lesson by writing the phrases "pesky purple parakeets", "two tangled turtles" and "lovely little lions" on the board. The new lesson will likely be about which of the following?
    a. Rhyming words
    b. Alliteration
    c. Word families
    d. Manipulation of syllables

23. Which of the following letters would be most beneficial to introduce after students can identify letter formations and shapes?
    a. Uppercase "B"
    b. Lowercase "s"
    c. Uppercase "R"
    d. Lowercase "p"

24. What area of study involves mechanics, usage, and sentence formation?
    a. Word analysis
    b. Spelling conventions
    c. Morphemes
    d. Phonics

25. What contributes the most to schema development?
    a. Reading comprehension
    b. Structural analysis
    c. Written language
    d. Background knowledge

26. What is the best way for a teacher to increase students' print awareness?
    a. Pointing to words as they are read
    b. Identifying words that rhyme while reading
    c. Emphasizing the root word within larger words
    d. Teaching the common word families

27. Syntax is best described as what?
    a. The arrangement of words in sentences
    b. The study of language meaning
    c. The study of grammar and language structure
    d. The proper formatting of a written text

28. What do informal reading assessments allow that standardized reading assessments do NOT allow?
    a. The application of grade-level norms toward a student's reading proficiency
    b. The personalization of reading assessments in order to differentiate instruction
    c. The avoidance of partialities in the interpretation of reading assessments
    d. The comparison of an individual's reading performance to that of other students in the class

29. The teacher presents a student with the word "dog" and asks them to identify which letter makes the /d/ sound. The student points to the letter "d". The teacher does the activity again with a few more sounds, and the student can accurately identify the letters that make each sound. What skill has the student mastered?
   a. Schwa sound
   b. Phonological awareness
   c. Alphabetic principle
   d. Word-analysis

30. A class has mastered CVC words. Which concept should the teacher introduce next?
   a. Short vowels
   b. Diphthongs
   c. Segmenting
   d. Consonant digraphs

31. Reading fluency is best described as the ability to do what?
   a. Read smoothly and accurately
   b. Comprehend what is read
   c. Demonstrate phonetic awareness
   d. Properly pronounce a list of words

32. A teacher writes the letters "S" and "R" on the board and says to the students "today we're going to learn about the letters 'S' and 'R'. S says /s/ as in 'snake', 'sit', and 'sun' and R says /r/ as in rain, run, and red." Which of the following best identifies which phonics teaching strategy they are using?
   a. Systematic instruction
   b. Recursive instruction
   c. Explicit instruction
   d. Reciprocal instruction

33. A teacher needs to assess students' accuracy in reading high frequency words and irregular sight words that are grade appropriate. Which of the following strategies would be most appropriate for this purpose?
   a. The teacher gives students a list of words to study for a spelling test that will be administered the following week.
   b. The teacher allows students to bring their favorite books from home and has them read their selected text aloud independently.
   c. The teacher administers the Stanford structural analysis assessment to determine students' rote memory and understanding of morphemes contained within the words.
   d. The teacher records how many words each student reads correctly when reading aloud a list of a teacher-selected, grade-appropriate words.

34. What type of texts are considered nonfiction?
   a. Folktales
   b. Memoirs
   c. Fables
   d. Short stories

35. The teacher provides a student with a list of words and asks them to pick out the words that contain diphthongs. The student identifies the following words correctly:
    a. Cow, boy, and sauce
    b. Pink, cat, and check
    c. Onion, green, and seal
    d. Frost, space, and tank

36. A teacher writes the word "unreachable" on the board and asks a student to come up and underline the affixes in the word. The student underlines "un" and "able". Which of the following best describes the focus of the lesson?
    a. Manipulation of syllables
    b. Onset and rime
    c. Morphological analysis
    d. Nuance of words

37. What do English learners (ELs) need to identify prior to comprehending text?
    a. Vocabulary
    b. Figurative language
    c. Author's purpose
    d. Setting

38. Which of the following scenarios is the MOST effective way to introduce irregular sight words to students?
    a. The teacher provides the student with flashcards with the sight words and helps them decode each one.
    b. The teacher provides the student with a paragraph that contains the sight words, and has the student read it independently.
    c. The teacher provides the student with a paper that has the sight words on them and has the student trace over each word as the teacher reads it aloud.
    d. The teacher provides the student with a list of the sight words and has them study it for homework.

39. A word that contains a syllable that ends in a single vowel follows which type of syllable pattern?
    a. Open
    b. Closed
    c. Final stable
    d. Vowel teams

40. A teacher writes the words *dice*, *mice*, and *nice* on the board and asks students what they have in common. A student replies that the three words all rhyme. The teacher agrees that the words do rhyme and notes that they share a similar spelling pattern, making them a part of the same _____.
    a. Word family
    b. Root word
    c. Base word
    d. Consonant digraph

41. A student can easily read the words *cat, in, stop, chug,* and *set.* However, the student struggles to read *kite, pie, bake,* and *rope.* Where should the teacher focus instruction next for this student?
   a. Vowel teams
   b. Consonant digraphs
   c. Long vowels
   d. Short vowels

42. What is "text evidence" when referring to answering a comprehension question?
   a. Taking phrases directly from the text itself to answer a question
   b. Using a variety of resources to find the answer
   c. Using technology and websites to locate an answer
   d. Paraphrasing and using a student's own words to answer the question

43. The words *star, clog,* and *crop* all contain a:
   a. Long vowel
   b. Diphthong
   c. Consonant digraph
   d. Consonant blend

44. Which of the following words contains the schwa sound?
   a. Banana
   b. Cheese
   c. Strawberry
   d. Egg

45. A student understands that letters and sounds make up words and can segment words and sound parts. The teacher says the word "crib" aloud and asks the student to write it on their paper. The student thinks and then writes the letters "c" "r" "i" "b" on their paper to write the word "crib". The student is practicing which of the following?
   a. Decoding
   b. Encoding
   c. Sight words
   d. Morphological analysis

46. A third-grade teacher notices that a few students are having trouble remembering their vocabulary words after she teaches them. What could she do during lessons to BEST help the students remember the words?
   a. Introduce each word one at a time by reading them from a list and writing them on the board, explaining each definition and having students take notes.
   b. Pass out a sheet with the vocabulary words and definitions and have students read them independently.
   c. Introduce one word at a time and have students write each word and its definition three times on their paper.
   d. Introduce one word at a time by writing them on the board and saying the definition, and have students think-pair-share with a partner to write their own definitions for the words.

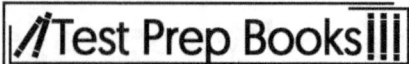

47. Which of the following can be useful when working with intervention groups of struggling readers?
    a. Having the teacher read aloud a text to the students while they take notes
    b. Having students read the text silently
    c. Assigning independent work and explaining the directions in detail
    d. Providing educational games for them to play while the teacher observes

48. What should be taught and mastered first when teaching reading comprehension?
    a. Theme
    b. Word analysis
    c. Text evidence
    d. Writing

49. Which of the following sentences contains an appositive?
    a. The otter swam away, never to be seen again.
    b. Tomatoes, the juicy red fruits, are my favorite food.
    c. I went to the store with Sally, Holly, and Hannah.
    d. I fell down, but then I got back on my feet.

50. When a student looks back at a previous reading section to help answer a question they have about the reading, he or she is using which of the following?
    a. Annotation
    b. KWL charts
    c. Metacognitive skills
    d. Directed reading-thinking activities

51. Before starting a new unit, a fifth-grade teacher introduces five new vocabulary words that students will need to understand for the upcoming lessons. Which of the following is the MOST effective technique to help students learn and remember the new words?
    a. Go over each word and its meaning, and then have students create sentences using the new words.
    b. Have students read a sample passage with the new words and have them guess what the words mean.
    c. Give the students a list of the new words and their definitions and have them read over it.
    d. Go over each new word and its meaning and give examples of synonyms and antonyms.

52. What is the spelling stage of a student who understands the correspondence between letters and sounds, but typically uses single letters to represent multiple sounds or syllables?
    a. Precommunicative stage
    b. Semi phonetic stage
    c. Phonetic stage
    d. Transitional stage

53. Most of the vocabulary words taught through literacy fall within which tier?
    a. Tier 1
    b. Tier 2
    c. Tier 3
    d. Tier 4

Practice Test

54. What are students utilizing when they ask themselves, "What do I know?", "What do I want to know?", and "What have I learned?" and record the answers in a table?
    a. Summarizing skills
    b. KWL charts
    c. Metacognitive skills
    d. T-charts

55. Tier 3 words should be taught:
    a. Explicitly as vocabulary words.
    b. Systematically at each new chapter.
    c. Prior to tier 2 words.
    d. Naturally as they appear in studies.

56. Bobby is reading a grade-level paragraph for a fluency check. He pronounces each word correctly but reads very quickly and doesn't pause to add emphasis or tone while reading. The teacher notes that Bobby is struggling with which of the following concepts?
    a. Prosody
    b. Accuracy
    c. Reading rate
    d. Nuance of words

57. A student is trying to decide if a character is telling the truth about having stolen candy. After the student reads that the character is playing with an empty candy wrapper in her pocket, the student decides the character is guilty. This is an example of what?
    a. Flashback
    b. Making inferences
    c. Text evidence
    d. Figurative language

58. A student can automatically read certain words at sight while reading through an unfamiliar text. This is an example of:
    a. Word identification
    b. Word recognition
    c. Structural analysis
    d. Context clues

59. A group of first-grade students are struggling with word identification. Which of the following techniques would BEST increase their word identification skills?
    a. Have the students practice writing their spelling words multiple times each.
    b. Play a matching game to pair words with matching pictures.
    c. Review the letters and letter sounds, as well as letter patterns like CVC words.
    d. Go over grammar rules like capitalization and punctuation.

60. The five basic elements of reading education are phonemic awareness, phonics, fluency, vocabulary, and which of the following?
    a. Spelling
    b. Comprehension
    c. Grammar
    d. Phoneme-grapheme correspondence

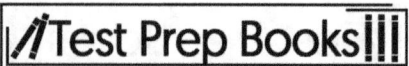

61. Which mode of writing aims to inform the reader objectively about a particular subject or idea and typically contains definitions, instructions, or facts within its subject matter?
    a. Argumentative
    b. Informative
    c. Narrative
    d. Descriptive

62. Editorials, letters of recommendation, and cover letters most likely incorporate which writing mode?
    a. Argumentative
    b. Informative
    c. Narrative
    d. Descriptive

63. After reading a passage on polar bears as a class, the teacher asks students to summarize what they just read. The teacher is primarily testing students on which of the following skills?
    a. Fluency
    b. Vocabulary
    c. Comprehension
    d. Decoding

64. Kimberly draws a picture of her family, and her instructor asks her to write what she drew on the line below the picture. She puts together a jumble of letter-like forms rather than a series of discrete letters. The instructor asks her what she wrote and she replies, "My family." Which stage of spelling development is Kimberly in?
    a. Pre-phonetic stage
    b. Semi phonetic stage
    c. Phonetic stage
    d. Conventional stage

65. When using Fry's formula to determine text complexity, what other factor should be considered?
    a. The number of sentences in each passage.
    b. The specific words used in the material.
    c. The number of syllables in each sentence.
    d. The amount of words in each sentence.

66. Which organizational style is used in the following passage?
    There are several reasons why the new student café has not been as successful as expected. One factor is that prices are higher than originally advertised, so many students cannot afford to buy food and beverages there. Also, the café closes rather early; as a result, students go out into town to other late-night gathering places rather than meeting friends at the café on campus.

    a. Cause and effect order
    b. Compare and contrast order
    c. Spatial order
    d. Time order

67. While reading independently, a student comes across the word "hyperextended" and is unfamiliar with its meaning. He knows that the root word *hyper* means "over" or "above" and connects that the word "hyperextended" must mean "to have over extended" something. Which independent strategy did the student use to define this unfamiliar word?
    a. Identification by origin
    b. Identification by synonym
    c. Identification by definition
    d. Identification by apposition

68. A student is interested in reading a short narrative story about a person seeing the Statue of Liberty for the first time, but she hasn't read about and doesn't know what the Statue of Liberty is. What should the teacher do?
    a. Recommend that the student pick out a different book because they are missing too much background knowledge.
    b. Have the student research the Statue of Liberty and write an essay on what it represents, then read the book.
    c. Explain the concept of the Statue of Liberty and show the student a few pictures, then have them read the book.
    d. Tell the student to ask a partner what the Statue of Liberty, and then read the book afterward.

69. Students can use context to identify unfamiliar words by:
    a. Looking up their definitions and meanings in multiple contexts.
    b. Coming up with examples of the unfamiliar words.
    c. Using the Greek or Latin root word to identify the word's meaning.
    d. Reading the text around the unfamiliar word to understand its' meaning.

70. Which type of words are students exposed to regularly through everyday conversations?
    a. Tier 1
    b. Tier 2
    c. Tier 3
    d. Tier 4

71. When reading a text independently, a student should highlight new vocabulary words and review their definitions:
    a. Prior to reading the text
    b. After reading the text
    c. When they appear naturally in the text
    d. With a partner to help further understanding

72. Practice activities like fill in the blanks, completing the end of a sentence, and describing the ending of a familiar story are best for building the vocabulary of students in which stage?
    a. Pre-literacy stage
    b. Early intermediate literacy stage
    c. Intermediate literacy stage
    d. Advanced literacy stage

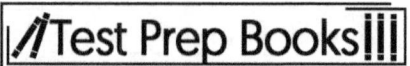

73. Which of the following techniques would BEST help build upon students' active listening skills?
    a. The teacher should assign each student a paragraph to read and summarize in one sentence, then share.
    b. The teacher should lead students in a directed drawing, where they must follow directions without a visual example.
    c. The teacher should introduce new vocabulary words and definitions and then have students practice using them in a sentence.
    d. The teacher should have students write down the questions they want to know before reading a story.

74. A first-grade teacher shows students the front cover of a book and the title before reading. Then, she asks students what it looks like is happening in the story based on the cover art. By doing this, the teacher is mainly trying to develop the students' _____.
    a. Summarizing skills
    b. Listening skills
    c. Comprehension skills
    d. Decoding skills

75. Which of the following writing activities supports reading comprehension?
    a. After reading a text about animal conservation, students construct a narrative essay about visiting a wildlife sanctuary.
    b. Students are assigned a persuasive essay on whether summer or winter is better.
    c. The class reads a novel together, and afterwards students write a paragraph summarizing the story.
    d. After the class reads an article on potato farming, students answer five multiple-choice questions to check for understanding.

76. Which of the following is true about informational text features?
    a. Indexes and glossaries are text features that help students find specific concepts in the text.
    b. Informational text features include transitional terms, use of alliteration, and text structure.
    c. All informational text contains text features that make it easier to navigate.
    d. Thesis statements are text features found in the beginning paragraph of a text.

77. While observing a second-grade student independently reading a book, the teacher noticed him saying "hm", "oh", and "wow" as he read. The student is practicing which of the following skills?
    a. Responsive reading
    b. Utilizing background knowledge
    c. Encoding
    d. Metacognition

78. Which of the following defines the stage of writing that involves adding to, removing, rearranging, or re-writing sections of a piece?
    a. The revising stage
    b. The publishing stage
    c. The writing stage
    d. The pre-writing stage

79. Which text type tells a true story or event in an engaging, short story style?
    a. Narrative
    b. Expository
    c. Literary nonfiction
    d. Procedural

80. Which of the following examples is a way that the teacher can differentiate instruction by process?
    a. The teacher can break students into groups by reading level and assign easier paragraphs to lower-level students.
    b. The teacher can give students the option to complete an assignment through an essay, art project, or speech.
    c. The teacher can allow students to read a story silently and then offer opportunities for students to act out the story.
    d. The teacher can provide an assessment in both English and Spanish.

81. A first grade teacher asks her students to write a sentence about an activity they did over the summer. One student, Amy, writes the following sentence: "I wnt to th bch." What stage of writing is Amy at?
    a. Pre-phonetic
    b. Semi-phonetic
    c. Phonetic
    d. Transitional

82. A teacher is looking for a program that will help him send out whole class messages, message specific parents, and add dates for tests and upcoming assignments. Which of the following would BEST help him accomplish this?
    a. Scribophile
    b. Turnitin
    c. Microsoft Word
    d. Remind

83. The teacher asks students to write a sentence about what they will do after school. Which of the following examples would be expected from a student in the pre-phonetic stage?
    a. JOT2RHSAK (Drawing of a swing set)
    b. GO OOTSID (Drawing of tree and sun)
    c. EET FUD (Drawing of a piece of pizza)
    d. I wil pla WTH my SiStr. (Drawing of two kids playing)

84. A student writes a first-person viewpoint essay on the best day they've ever had. Which type of writing is this classified as?
    a. Fictional narrative
    b. Nonfiction narrative
    c. Expository
    d. Opinion

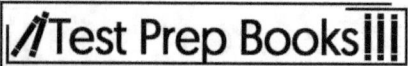

85. A basic rule of syntax is that sentences generally follow which order?
    a. Subject-object-verb
    b. Verb-object-subject
    c. Subject-verb-object
    d. Object-verb-subject

86. Mr. Rodriguez notices that one of his students, Sam, always starts sentences with a lowercase letter. He has already taught a lesson on capitalization and most of the class uses capitalization correctly. What is the best way to handle this situation?
    a. Mr. Rodriguez should reteach the lesson on capitalization as a reminder.
    b. Mr. Rodriguez should assign Sam extra homework assignments on capitalization.
    c. Mr. Rodriguez should correct Sam's work with capital letters and have a conversation with Sam about when to use capitalization.
    d. Mr. Rodriguez should wait and give Sam a chance to start using capitalization in his writing.

87. In which spelling stage are students ready to begin learning about homophones?
    a. Semi-phonetic
    b. Phonetic
    c. Transitional
    d. Conventional

88. Roger has been teaching his kindergarten class new words and story structure. He uses poems and music that are focused on characters having adventures. The stories often rhyme, and the children in his class thoroughly enjoy them. What type of story is Roger using to teach his class?
    a. Myths
    b. Fairy tales
    c. Nursery rhymes
    d. Folklore

89. A teacher is covering a lesson on annotation and wants to show her students an example. Which of the following examples BEST shows annotation?
    a. The teacher reads a story aloud and asks students which words they find challenging.
    b. The teacher reads a story aloud and then asks students to explain what happened in the story.
    c. The teacher reads the story aloud and pauses to ask students what they think will happen next.
    d. The teacher reads the story aloud and makes notes of important details on the board.

90. A student successfully spells the words "popcorn", "milk", and "chair" but struggles to spell "what", "eyes", and "friend". Which stage of spelling is the student in?
    a. Transitional
    b. Phonetic
    c. Conventional
    d. Semi phonetic

Assessment and Instructional Decision Making

When preparing for the constructed response section of the test, it is important to identify what the scenario is asking you to analyze and to make sure that your ideas are organized. Typically, a constructed response question will give you a scenario to analyze. The scenario will pertain to the science of teaching reading. Additionally, the question will include the information it wants you to specifically address in your response, as well as some additional information that could assist you in constructing your response.

There will be three constructed response questions on the test and each question will be scored on a scale of 0-3.

To earn a score of 3, the response must entirely and specifically answer every part of the question and scenario presented. It should include any relevant theories, concepts, or methods used in teaching reading that apply to the situation. The response should be strongly supported by facts and evidence pulled directly from the scenario.

A score of 2 is awarded when the test taker answers most of the question and scenario presented to them. The response should include general theories and concepts that have to do with teaching reading, and there should be some supporting evidence for the claims made.

A score of 1 is given if the response answers just part or a few parts of the question, but either: fails to answer with an appropriate response or displays no knowledge (or inaccurate knowledge) of facts and evidence related to teaching reading.

A score of 0 is given if the response answer doesn't respond to any part of the question or scenario at all. Responses made in other languages, answers that are completely unrelated, or blank responses will also earn a 0.

On the test, you may be asked to construct a response based on the follow concepts:

- **Developing Emergent Literacy Learners**
  - Phonological and Phonemic Awareness
  - Phonics
  - Decoding/Encoding
- **Supporting Independent Literacy Learners**
  - Fluency
  - Vocabulary
  - Comprehension
  - Writing
- Responding to Diverse Learners
  - Gifted
  - English Learners
  - Struggling Reads and Writers
  - Students with Learning Disabilities

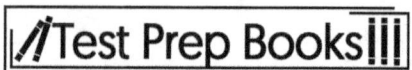

Assessment and Instructional Decision Making

Constructed Response Question

Prepare an Organized Written Response to a Topic Relating to the Development of Student Literacy.

Scenario: Mr. Brown is a reading specialist at Carroll High School and assists several teachers and classes with literacy development skills. While most students seem to be writing well, Mr. Brown notices that several students in the classes seem to have trouble reading written words. These children come from a wide range of backgrounds, including native and non-native English speakers.

Task 1: What are some ways Mr. Brown can assess the students' skill levels to determine where the root of their reading issues lie?

Task 2: Describe how Mr. Brown can guide the instructors in addressing the reading issues with differentiated instruction.

Sample Response (Score of 3)

Task 1: To uncover the root of the reading issues, Mr. Brown will need to assess students' skill levels, and one manner of doing so is through determining their Lexile reading levels. To determine their reading levels, the students should be given a standardized reading comprehension assessment. The most used Lexile measure assessment is the Scholastic Reading Inventory, which matches students to a reading level that corresponds with books and other texts. The results from the assessment will show exactly which areas the student has trouble in, which should identify the root of their reading issues.

In addition to determining the students' Lexile reading levels, Mr. Brown or the classroom teacher can conduct a Developmental Reading Assessment (DRA) on each student. As the reading specialist, Mr. Brown should select one standard passage or short story for the entire grade level, making the assessment standardized. Then, either Mr. Brown or the classroom teacher should individually assess students by having them read the passage aloud, making notes when the student misses words or makes mistakes. Afterwards, the student will retell the story, and the instructor should note any gaps in reading comprehension. This assessment allows Mr. Brown to identify the specific reading issues that students have like difficulty with phoneme-grapheme correspondence or blending, and get to the root of any problems that exist.

Task 2: Mr. Brown can guide instructors in differentiating the content and process of student learning. One example that Mr. Brown can offer to instructors is to change the content that students are learning. Since it's evident that some students are struggling to read words, the content can be modified by using simpler language and easier words. First, the students should be broken into groups based on their reading levels which were assessed through Lexile measures or the DRA (or both). Then, the groups that have lower reading levels should be assigned the same, standard reading activities, but they should be modified to use simpler language. During this time, teachers can also meet with the leveled groups to focus on specific remediation skills that each group needs.

Another idea that Mr. Brown can share with the teachers is to differentiate the process of student learning. Since many students have trouble reading written words, teachers can offer opportunities for students to learn through audio books, visual guides and charts, or videos. Differentiating the content and process that students learn in encourages the success of all readers.

Commentary on Sample Response (Score of 3)

This response entirely and accurately answers the two tasks which are presented in the question. In the first task, the test taker notes two ways to test for reading skills and offers detailed and specific instructions on how to do so and the material to use. The response identifies how Mr. Brown will be able to identify the root causes of student reading issues through two methods of determining their reading skill levels. In task 2, the test taker accurately describes two methods for differentiating instruction: by process and content. They provide specific examples of differentiation and how the instructors can use differentiation to address the student reading issues.

Sample Response (Score of 2)

Mr. Brown can assess the students' reading skill levels in a few different ways. First, he could have students take a Lexile measure assessment to test for their Lexile reading level. Additionally, he can have students take a Developmental Reading Assessment (DRA) that requires students to read a standard passage and then retell what happened to the instructor. While the student reads, Mr. Brown should take notes and identify any areas where the student is having reading trouble.

Mr. Brown can also help teachers use differentiated instruction to address the student reading issues. Since many students struggle with reading words, he can suggest that the teacher try differentiating the material that the students use to make the words simpler. This way, the teacher could break students into groups by reading level and give the same assignment to each, but modify the words to be easier for some groups. Mr. Brown can also suggest that teachers offer students the opportunity to learn through different ways other than just written text.

Commentary on Sample Response (Score of 2)

This response answers most of the question in at a general level, but fails to provide as many specific examples as the response that scored a 3. In task 1, the test taker accurately describes two ways to test for students' reading skills, but doesn't include how those assessments can identify the root causes of the reading issues. In task 2, the test taker includes specific examples of differentiating instruction to assess student reading issues. However, it doesn't include specific examples of ways that students can learn other than written text.

Sample Response (Score of 1)

Mr. Brown can have teachers test students on their reading skills to find out where the problems are. The teachers could have each student read the same passage and then explain what happened in the story. Mr. Brown should talk to the teachers about the areas that the students struggle in and how they can support those specific areas. Some of the students may be struggling with letter and sound correspondence and the other students may be having different issues. Having students take a standardized assessment will show how they do compared to the rest of the class.

Commentary on Sample Response (Score of 1)

This response answers very little of the question in a general level. It addresses task 1 in terms of testing student reading levels but doesn't provide any specific examples or ideas. The response doesn't address task 2 at all. This response shows that the test taker has very limited knowledge to answer the question.

Assessment and Instructional Decision Making

Sample Constructed Response Questions

The constructed response questions on the exam will usually present a situation and require the test taker to respond with two tasks. It's important that both tasks are adequately responded to in detail and entirely. The following are examples of constructed response questions that may appear on the exam:

The following case study is focused on Caleb, a second-grade student.

Caleb's primary instructor has noticed that when Caleb reads material aloud in class, he will often take long pauses and read the sentences slower than the other students. This sometimes causes him to stutter or hesitate during longer sentences. Despite this, Caleb is very bright and seems to fully grasp the context of the material. He also appears to be engaged when answering questions but is hesitant when having to read in front of the class.

Caleb's teacher has requested that Mr. Breiner, the reading specialist, evaluate Caleb to understand what might be causing his issues. Mr. Breiner has been requested to present ideas on how to help Caleb's reading skills improve. The teacher wants to be able to learn how to address reading issues like Caleb's in the future, or at least be able to identify core literary issues very early in the developmental stage.

The teacher notes the following:

- When reading the sentence, "The next-door neighbors adopted the cat that had been homeless," Caleb switched *the* and *cat*. He also seemed to take longer to sound out *homeless*.
- Longer sentences seem to cause Caleb confusion when reading aloud.
- In some of his writing responses, Caleb will sometimes switch the letters within the words or the words themselves.
- Caleb understands material clearly and gives insightful thoughts aloud. No speech problems were observed.

Task 1: Identify methods of observation that may indicate whether or not Caleb has a diverse learning profile. What kind of assessments can be used to determine if his reading difficulties are tied to specific written English structures or if his pausing indicates other disconnects?

Task 2: Based on Caleb's learning profile, what are some teaching strategies that can be used to help him improve? Provide details on why differentiating Caleb's instruction would be a major step in bolstering his reading ability.

The following case study is focused on Ms. Pearson, a fifth-grade social studies teacher.

Ms. Pearson, a fifth-grade social studies teacher, has a class that reads at various levels. About half of her class is critically below grade level by over a year, and they struggle to read independently and recall the information. Five of her students are completely fluent in reading and have no trouble comprehending the materials in the social studies textbook. Another five students are just below grade level in reading and need some support while reading the social studies materials.

- Task 1: Describe two specific methods of differentiation that Ms. Pearson can use to support the needs of her students. Include information on specific methods for differentiating for lower and higher-level students.

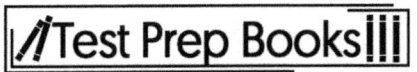

- Task 2: Identify specific ways that Ms. Pearson can group students to support differentiation and address each students' specific reading needs.

Answer Explanations

1. A: The *sh* is an example of a consonant digraph. Consonant digraphs are combinations of two or three consonants that work together to make a single sound. Examples of consonant digraphs are *sh*, *ch*, and *th*. Choice *B*, sound segmentation, is used to identify component phonemes in a word, such as separating the /t/, /u/, and /b/ in tub. Choice *C*, vowel team (or diphthong), is a set of two vowels that make up a single sound, such as *ow*, *ae*, or *ie*. Choice *D*, rime, is the sound that follows a word's onset, such as the /at/ in *cat*.

2. D: Phoneme segmentation is the identification of all the component phonemes in a word. An example would be the student identifying each separate sound, /t/, /u/, and /b/, in the word *tub*. Choice *A*, sound blending, is the blending together of two or more sounds in a word, such as /ch/ or /sh/. Choice *B*, substitution, occurs when a phoneme is substituted within a word for another phoneme, such as substituting the sound /b/ in *bun* to /r/ to create *run*. Choice *C*, rhyming, is an effective tool to utilize during the analytic phase of phonics development because rhyming words are often identical except for their beginning letters.

3. A: The alphabetic principle is the understanding that letters represent sounds in words. It is through the alphabetic principle that students learn the interrelationships between letter-sound (grapheme-phoneme) correspondences, phonemic awareness, and early decoding skills (such as sounding out and blending letter sounds).

4. D: Print awareness includes all the answer choices except the spelling of sight words. Print awareness includes Choice *A*, the differentiation of uppercase and lowercase letters, so that students can understand which words begin a sentence. Choice *B*, the identification of word boundaries, is also included in print awareness; that is, students should be made aware that words are made up of letters and that spaces appear between words, etc. Choice *C*, the proper tracking of words, is also included in print awareness, which is the realization that print is organized in a particular way, so books must be tracked and held accordingly.

5. A: The correct answer is phonological awareness, the understanding that words are made of multiple sounds working together, which aids with rhyming abilities. Phoneme deletion includes deleting letters or parts of a word, phoneme blending is the ability to blend letters to create words, and directionality is the ability to track words while reading.

6. B: Structural analysis focuses on the meaning of morphemes. Morphemes include base words, prefixes, and word endings (inflections and suffixes) that are found within longer words. Students can use structural analysis skill to find familiar word parts within an unfamiliar word in order to decode the word and determine the definition of the new word. The prefix *im-* (meaning not) in the word *improbable* can help students derive the definition of an event that is not likely to occur.

7. B: The student is performing at the phonetic stage. Phonetic spellers will spell a word as it sounds. The speller perceives and represents all the phonemes in a word. However, because phonetic spellers have limited sight word vocabulary, irregular words are often spelled incorrectly.

Answer Explanations

8. B: The correct answer is phoneme deletion, which is the ability to remove phonemes to create a new word. The students understood phoneme-grapheme correspondence and blending because they were able to read the original word but struggled to understand deletion. Phoneme substitution would have involved substituting a different phoneme for the "s" rather than removing it completely.

9. D: The best choice of letter for her next lesson is "s". The lowercase "d" and "p" letters are too visually similar to "b", and "v" is too similar in letter sound. "S" is the best choice because it doesn't look or sound like "b".

10. C: Because the student can follow directions, but isn't able to verbally express herself, she has receptive language skills. Expressive language skills would include an ability to respond with words or gestures, and basic and auditory language skills are both fictitious answer choices.

11. C: Writing samples are the most appropriate assessment of spelling for students who are performing at the pre-phonetic stages. During this stage, students participate in pre-communicative writing, which appears to be a jumble of letter-like forms rather than a series of discrete letters. Samples of students' pre-communicative writing can be used to assess their understanding of the alphabetic principle and their knowledge of letter-sound correspondences.

12. A: Phonological awareness is best assessed through identification of rimes or onsets within words. Instruction of phonological awareness includes detecting and identifying word boundaries, onsets/rimes, syllables, and rhyming words.

13. A: The identification of morphemes within words occurs during the instruction of structural analysis. Structural analysis is a word recognition skill that focuses on the meanings of word parts, or morphemes, during the introduction of a new word. Choice *B*, syllabic analysis, is a word analysis skill that helps students split words into syllables. Choice *C*, phonics, is the direct correspondence between and blending of letters and sounds. Choice *D*, the alphabetic principle, teaches that letters or other characters represent sounds.

14. B: The correct answer is segmenting because the child was able to take the whole word and break it into its individual phonemes. Blending is the opposite of segmenting, which involves taking individual phonemes and reading them as a whole word. Manipulations of syllables and substitution both involve replacing the syllables and phonemes in words with other letters.

15. B: Nursery rhymes are used in kindergarten to develop phoneme recognition. Rhyming words are often almost identical except for their beginning letter(s), so rhyming is a great strategy to implement during the analytic phase of phoneme development.

16. B: High-frequency words are taught during the instruction of sight word recognition. Sight words, sometimes referred to as high-frequency words, are words that are used often but may not follow the regular principles of phonics. Sight words may also be defined as words that students are able to recognize and read without having to sound out.

17. A: Fill in the blank activities are best for learners at the early intermediate stage because they are still working to understand vocabulary and how to form sentences. Silent reading, partner-shared reading, and word web activities are all too advanced for learners at the early intermediate literacy stage.

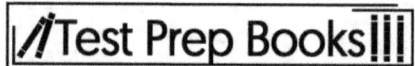

18. D: The correct answer is Choice *D*, the teacher should have Samantha read the same passage multiple times to help her read accurately, smoothly, and fluently. Choice *A* is incorrect because fluency aims to reduce the amount of times a student stops while reading. Choice *B* is incorrect because fluency is best supported by practicing the same passage multiple times instead of changing the passage. Choice *C* is incorrect because understanding of genre doesn't affect fluency.

19. A: There is a positive correlation between a student's exposure to text and an increase in their written vocabulary. Therefore, students should be given ample opportunities to read independently as much text as possible in order to gain vocabulary and background knowledge.

20. C: By definition, morphology is the identification and use of morphemes such as root words and affixes. Listening comprehension refers to the processes involved in understanding spoken language. Word consciousness refers to the knowledge required for students to learn and effectively utilize language. Textual analysis is an approach that researchers use to gain information and describe the characteristics of a recorded or visual message.

21. B: The best choice of graphic organizer for showing cause-and-effect relationships is a t-chart. Venn diagrams are best used to compare and contrast topics, KWL charts are best used before and after reading to determine understanding, and spider maps are best used for brainstorming ideas about a single topic or project.

22. B: The correct answer is alliteration, which is when two or more words in a phrase begin with the same sound or sound group. Rhyming words and manipulation of syllables both require words to have the same ending sounds, and word families also usually share the same ending sounds.

23. C: Uppercase letters should be introduced before lowercase letters, eliminating Choices B and D, and continuous sounds (like the letter 'R') should be taught before stop sounds (like the letter 'B'), making Choice C the correct answer.

24. B: Spelling conventions is the area of study that involves mechanics, usage, and sentence formation. Mechanics refers to spelling, punctuation, and capitalization. Usage refers to the use of the various parts of speech within sentences, and sentence formation is the order in which the various words in a sentence appear. Generally speaking, word analysis is the breaking down of words into morphemes and word units in order to arrive at the word's meaning.

25. D: A schema is a framework or structure that stores and retrieves multiple, interrelated learning elements as a single packet of knowledge. Children who have greater exposure to life events have greater schemas. Thus, students who bring extensive background knowledge to the classroom are likely to experience easier automation when reading. In this way, background knowledge and reading comprehension are directly related. Likewise, students who have greater background knowledge can learn a greater number of new concepts at a faster rate.

26. A: The teacher should point to words while reading to encourage understanding of one-to-one correspondence and directionality, two key aspects of print awareness. Identifying rhyming words will increase phonological awareness, and both root words and word families are phonics skills.

27. A: Syntax refers to the arrangement of words and phrases to form properly flowing sentences and paragraphs. Semantics has to do with language meaning. Grammar is a composite of all systems and structures utilized within a language and includes syntax, word morphology, semantics, and phonology.

Cohesion and coherence of oral and written language are promoted through a full understanding of syntax, semantics, and grammar.

28. B: Informal reading assessments allow teachers to create differentiated assessments that target reading skills of individual students. In this way, teachers can gain insight into a student's reading strengths and weaknesses. Informal assessments can help teachers decide what content and strategies need to be targeted. However, standardized reading assessments provide all students with the same structure to assess multiple skills at one time. Standardized reading assessments cannot be individualized. Such assessments are best used for gaining an overview of student reading abilities.

29. C: The student has mastered the alphabetic principle and understands phoneme-grapheme correspondence (the understanding that letters correspond with specific sounds). The schwa sound is the vowel sound in a word that isn't emphasized, which usually sounds like "uh". Phonological awareness refers to an understanding of rhyming words and the knowledge that words can be broken into parts. Word analysis is the ability to recognize the relationships between new and unfamiliar words.

30. D: After mastery of CVC words, the teacher should introduce consonant digraphs. Short vowels and segmenting have already been mastered, and diphthongs should be taught after mastery of blends and digraphs.

31. A: Reading fluency is the ability to accurately read at a socially acceptable pace and with proper expression. Phonetic awareness leads to the proper pronunciation of words and fluency. Once students can read fluently, concentration is no longer dedicated toward the process of reading. Instead, students can concentrate on the meaning of a text. Thus, in the developmental process of reading, comprehension follows fluency.

32. C: The teacher is using explicit instruction to teach phonics because the lesson is entirely teacher-led and accurately modeled, rather than student-led, as recursive instruction usually is. Systematic instruction requires gradual teaching and only focusing on one sound at a time. Reciprocal instruction is a fictitious answer choice.

33. D: The teacher records how many words each student reads correctly when reading aloud a list of a teacher-selected, grade-appropriate words. Accuracy is measured as the percentage of words that are read correctly within a given text. Word-reading accuracy is often measured by counting the number of errors that occur per 100 words of oral reading. This information is used to select the appropriate level of text for an individual.

34. B: Nonfiction texts include memoirs, biographies, autobiographies, and journalism. Choices *A*, *C*, and *D* are all examples of fictional prose.

35. A: The only words that contain diphthongs are cow, boy, and sauce. All the other examples include consonant blends or digraphs, and "io", "ee" and "ea" are not examples of diphthongs.

36. C: Morphological analysis is the ability to break words into multiple parts by their affixes and root/base words. Manipulation of syllables would require the student to change syllables in the word to create a new word. Onset and rime refer to the parts of a word that make it rhyme with other words. Nuance of words is the different meanings a word may have in different contexts.

37. A: English learners (ELs) should master vocabulary and word usages to fully comprehend text. Figurative language, an author's purpose, and settings are more complex areas and are difficult for

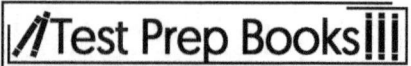

Answer Explanations

English learners (ELs). These areas can be addressed once EL students understand the meanings of words. To master comprehension skills, vocabulary and the English language need to be mastered first, but comprehension can still be difficult. Figurative language is culture-based, and inferences may be difficult for those with a different cultural background.

38. C: One of the most effective ways for teaching irregular sight words is through rainbow writing, or having students trace over the words to learn how to write them. Choice A is incorrect because irregular words are not decodable. Choice B is incorrect because the student likely won't be able to read the sight words independently yet. Choice D is incorrect because the student can't practice words independently that they don't know.

39. A: A word that ends in a single vowel, like "go", "to", or "by", follows an open syllable pattern. A word that follows a closed pattern would contain a consonant and single vowel followed by another consonant. Final stable syllables are syllables that can be recognized at the end of many words, like *cious, sion,* and *age.* Vowel team patterns are when words have two consecutive vowels, like "moon", "bait", and "boil".

40. A: Each of these words are a part of the same word family because they share a similar spelling and sound pattern. While some word families share the same root words and base words, that is not the case with the "ice" family. Consonant digraphs are when two consonants are put together to create a single sound.

41. C: The student can successfully read words with short vowels and consonant digraphs but struggles with CVCV words and long vowels. Vowel teams, or diphthongs, should be taught after long vowels are learned.

42. A: "Text evidence" refers to taking phrases and sentences directly from the text and writing them in the answer. Students are not asked to paraphrase, nor use any other resources to address the answer. Therefore, Choices B, C, and D are incorrect.

43. D: Each of these words contain a consonant blend (*st, cl, cr*). They do not contain long vowels, diphthongs, or consonant digraphs.

44. A: The schwa sound is a sound that any unstressed vowel can make, and it sounds like the short /u/ sound. The word "banana" makes the schwa sound twice at "buh" and "nuh". The word "cheese", "strawberry", and "egg" do not contain the schwa sound.

45. B: The student is encoding, or spelling, the word. Decoding, or reading, is the opposite of encoding. Sight words are words that student practice reading by sight, and morphological analysis is breaking a word into parts to analyze its meaning.

46. D: The best way to embed vocabulary words in students' memory is through exposure to the word multiple times in multiple contexts, in a way that students can make their own personal connections to the words. Working with a partner to create new definitions for the vocabulary words and reading/hearing the actual words and definitions allows for exposure in multiple contexts. Rote memorization, as in Choice C, is not nearly as successful for memorization. Choice A is incorrect because third-grade students may not take the correct notes and there is no personal connection made to the words. Choice B is incorrect because introduction to new vocabulary words should be primarily teacher-led because students may not fully understand the definitions if done independently.

Answer Explanations

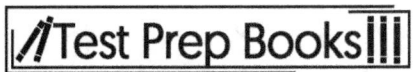

47. A: Small intervention groups can benefit from a teacher reading a text or small book aloud while students listen and take notes. This helps struggling students to focus on reading comprehension rather than having to decode words. Intervention time is not meant for a teacher to give independent work nor to just provide observation without support, and while educational games are fun, they aren't as effective in supporting reading comprehension as teacher-led reading and student notetaking.

48. B: Word analysis (which leads to fluency) should be mastered before teaching theme, text evidence, and writing. For English learners (ELs) and struggling readers, word analysis and fluency are often difficult barriers, which is why comprehension skills are not initially mastered. Theme is often a complex and inferential skill, which is developed later. Text evidence is pulling answers to comprehension questions directly from a text and cannot be accomplished until readers can fluently read and understand the text. Writing skills generally come after comprehension skills are underway.

49. B: Appositives are words that define or add meaning to a term that directly precedes them, usually occurring with a comma on each side of the appositives. Choices *A, C,* and *D* are incorrect.

50. C: Asking oneself a comprehension question is a metacognitive skill. Readers with metacognitive skills have learned to think about their thinking. It gives students control over their learning while they read. KWL charts help students to identify what they already know about a given topic, annotation requires the student to highlight or take notes, and directed reading-thinking activities are teacher-led.

51. A: The best way for students to learn new vocabulary is by using it in multiple settings. Having students create their own sentences using the new words after introduction by the teacher is a researched-based technique for learning new vocabulary.

52. B: During the semi phonetic stage, students begin to understand letter-sound correspondences and can begin using letters to create words. However, students will usually spell words incorrectly according to how they sound rather than following typical grammar rules, and often vowels are forgotten or omitted (for example, "dnts" for "donuts" or "U" for "you".

53. B: Most of the vocabulary words that are taught in literacy or reading fall within Tier 2, which consists of common words that are used in many subjects.

54. B: KWL charts are effective methods of activating prior knowledge and taking advantage of students' curiosity. Students can create a KWL (know/want to know/learned) chart to prepare for any unit of instruction and to generate questions about a topic.

55. D: Tier 3 words are content-specific and should be taught as they come up naturally, through text, independent reading, and other studies.

56. A: Bobby is struggling with prosody, because although he can accurately read words at a quick reading rate, he isn't pausing to add expression, emphasis, and tone while reading.

57. B: Making inferences is a method of deriving meaning that is intended by the author but not explicitly stated in the text. A flashback is a scene set earlier than the main story. Text evidence is informational pulled directly from the text rather than inferred. Figurative language is text that is not to be taken literally.

58. B: Word recognition is the ability to correctly and automatically recognize words at sight, without needing to stop and decode them. Word identification is the ability to decode words using strategies.

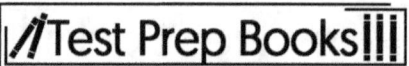

Structural analysis includes breaking words into parts, and context clues would involve using surrounding text to understand word meaning.

59. C: Word identification is the ability to sound out a word using decoding strategies. The best way to increase word identification skills is by teaching phoneme-grapheme correspondence and word structure including letter patterns.

60. B: The five basic components of reading education are phonemic awareness, phonics, fluency, vocabulary, and comprehension.

61. B: The key word here is inform, which is the primary purpose of all informative modes. They contain facts, definitions, instructions, and other elements with the objective purpose of informing a reader—such as study guides, instruction manuals, and textbooks. Choice A is incorrect because an argumentative mode contains language that is subjective and is intended to persuade or to inform with a persuasive bias. Choice C is incorrect as a narrative mode is used primarily to tell a story and has no intention of informing, nor is the language inherently objective. Choice D is incorrect as descriptive modes possess no inherent intent to inform and are used primarily to describe.

62. A: Editorials, recommendation letters, and cover letters all seek to persuade a reader to agree with the author, which reflects an argumentative mode. Choice B is incorrect because the intent of the above examples is to persuade a reader to agree with the author, not to present information. Choice C is incorrect as the above examples are not trying to tell a story. Choice D is also incorrect because while the above examples may contain many descriptions, that is not their primary purpose.

63. C: The ability to summarize a text is indicative of a student's reading comprehension abilities.

64. A: Kimberly is in the pre-phonetic stage of spelling because she formed a jumble of letter-like forms rather than a series of discrete letters. This indicates she has pre-communicative writing ability only. Her letter-sound correspondence is limited. In the semi-phonetic stage, she would have demonstrated a better understanding of the fact that letters represent sounds. She may have missed syllables in her words or used single letters to represent entire words, but she would have demonstrated letter formation and the alphabetic principle. The other choices list stages in which her spelling would be even further advanced.

65. B: When using Fry's formula, it's important for teachers to skim the text to review the specific words used in the material. That's because the formula rates texts based on sentence length, including syllables and words. It doesn't account for the specific words that are used, so obscure words that have few syllables may make a text appear easier than it truly is.

66. A: The passage describes a situation and then explains the causes that led to it. Also, it utilizes cause and effect signal words, such as *reasons*, *factors*, *so*, and *as a result*. Choice B is incorrect because a compare and contrast order considers the similarities and differences of two or more things. Choice C is incorrect because spatial order describes where things are located in relation to each other. Finally, Choice D is incorrect because time order describes when things occurred chronologically.

67. A: This is an example of identification by origin because the student was able to give meaning to the unfamiliar word based on his knowledge of the word's origin and root word.

68. C: If the background knowledge necessary for reading a book isn't too complicated, the teacher should explain the background to the student and then have them read the book. The teacher shouldn't

Answer Explanations

tell them to pick a different book (Choice A) unless the student lacks significant, important background knowledge that would take a lot of time to learn. In this case, independent study (Choice B) and asking a partner (Choice D) will not ensure that the student gets an accurate knowledge of background information.

69. D: Students can use the context of a word, or where it is used in relation to other text around it, to understand the meaning of unfamiliar words. The other choices are strategies for defining unfamiliar words by definition, example, and origin.

70. A: Tier 1 words are also called common words because they are in everyday conversation. Tier 2 words are mainly used in academic settings and conversations, and tier 3 words are content-specific words that are rarely used in conversation. Tier 4 does not exist.

71. A: Before reading a text independently, it's important for the student to highlight and review the definitions of new vocabulary words to avoid becoming distracted during reading or reducing fluency. All other answer choices are incorrect.

72. B: Fill in the blank activities, sentence completion and describing the end of a familiar stories are great activities for students in the early intermediate literacy stage. The pre-literacy stage is not a real stage of literacy, and these activities would be too simple for learners in the intermediate or advanced literacy stages.

73. B: The best way to improve students' listening comprehension is by having them practice following directions, listening to stories, and conversing. Therefore, Choice B is the correct answer because it requires students to actively listen without any other cues. The other answers require more reading, writing, or speaking than listening.

74. C: The teacher is trying to improve students' comprehension skills by asking questions to get them thinking about the meaning and the events of the story. By first thinking about what the text could be about, the students are now interested and able to increase their comprehension as the story is read.

75. C: The correct answer is Choice C because it is the only option that requires students to write using their reading comprehension skills. Choice A is incorrect because a narrative essay is a story, and writing about visiting a wildlife sanctuary doesn't require them to have understood the text on animal conservation. Choice B is incorrect because there is no reading involved, although it is a writing activity. Choice D is incorrect because, although it supports reading comprehension, answering multiple-choice questions isn't a writing activity.

76. A: Indexes and glossaries are a type of text feature, along with titles and subtitles, italics and bold print, and visual features like diagrams. Therefore, Choice B is incorrect. While most informational text includes text features, not all informational text does. A thesis statement is not a text feature, and it is not always found in the beginning paragraph.

77. D: The student is practicing metacognition by verbally responding to the text he is reading silently. Verbal cues help to keep readers aware of their own thought processes as they read.

78. A: The revising stage involves adding, removing, and rearranging sections of a written work. Choice B is incorrect as the publishing stage involves the distribution of the finished product to the publisher, teacher, or reader. Choice C is incorrect because the writing stage is the actual act of writing the work,

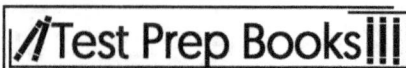

and generally does not including editing or revision. Choice D is incorrect as the pre-writing stage involves the planning, drafting, and researching of the intended piece.

79. C: Literary nonfiction, or creative nonfiction, is the most common type of informational text. It tells a true story based on facts in the style of an engaging short story.

80. C: The correct answer is Choice C because differentiating instruction by process means modifying the way that students learn. In this example, students have the opportunity to learn the information through reading as well as kinesthetically through acting out the story. Choices A and D both differentiate the instruction by content rather than process. Choice B differentiates instruction by product.

81. B: Amy is at the semi-phonetic stage of writing. She understands that letters denote specific sounds (WNT for 'went'; BCH for 'beach'). However, she still omits multiple syllables within the words and leaves out spaces. The pre-phonetic stage happens before this; the child doesn't understand that letters make specific sounds and words. In the phonetic stage of writing, children spell words according to how they sound without focusing on correct spelling ("kat" instead of "cat"). The transitional stage of writing occurs when children can write a clear sentence with correct grammar, spelling, and punctuation.

82. D: Remind is the best program that will allow the teacher to accomplish all of these tasks. Scribophile, Turnitin, and Microsoft Word are all focused on writing and publishing rather than communication.

83. A: The pre-phonetic stage is the first, most basic stage of writing. At this stage, students do not know letter-sound correspondences and will produce an abstract jumble of letters or letter shapes, therefore Choice A is correct. Choices B and C exhibit responses from semi-phonetic students because the samples show the beginnings of letter-sound correspondence. Choice D is an example of the phonetic stage, as all words are spelled phonetically even if not accurately.

84. B: A first-person viewpoint makes the essay a narrative, and since it is based on true events and facts rather than made-up details, it is considered nonfiction narrative.

85. C: Most sentences follow the subject-verb-object format. For example, Gus (subject) played (verb) baseball (object). Sentences don't easily make sense when the order of any of these is swapped.

86. C: The best way to handle this situation is by correcting the lowercase letter to a capital and having a conversation with the student, Sam. Since the rest of the class doesn't seem to struggle with capitalization, reteaching it to the whole group is unnecessary. Assigning extra homework or waiting for the student to start using capitalization are both less effective responses.

87. A: Students are ready to begin learning homophones at the transitional stage of spelling. At this stage, students should have a deep understanding of letter-sound correspondences and greater accuracy when spelling irregular words.

88. C: Nursery rhymes are poems or songs that teach children new terms and stories. Choice A is incorrect; myths are stories told to attempt to explain the origin of something. Choice B is incorrect because while fairy tales can be as entertaining as nursery rhymes, they are not sung; they are short stories that sometimes contain supernatural elements. Choice D is incorrect because folklore are orated stories about common people.

Answer Explanations

89. D: The only example that includes annotation is Choice *D* because the teacher is reading and showing how to take notes. Choice *A* helps students to think about the difficult words in the story, but it misses the element of underlining or note taking. Choice *B* covers the concept of summarizing and Choice *C* is an example of making predictions.

90. A: The student is in the transitional stage because they are able to spell conventionally spelled words correctly but cannot spell many irregularly spelled words.

Index

A Five-Finger Retell Activity, 43
Accuracy, 35, 38
Active Learning, 59, 60
Advanced Literacy Stage, 14
Affix, 23
Alliteration, 12, 52
Analytic, 94, 95
Anchor Charts, 64
Annotation, 65
Antagonist, 50
Appositives, 32
Auditory Learning, 59
Autobiography, 50, 67
Background Knowledge, 32, 33, 40, 41, 42, 43, 96
Base Words, 23
Biographies and Autobiographies, 50
Biography, 16, 50
Blending, 12
Cause/Effect, 54
Central Or Major Characters, 50
Characters, 50
Chronological/Sequence Order, 54
Collaborative Learning, 59
Comedy, 50
Communication, 57, 66
Comparison/Contrast, 54
Conflict, 51
Consonant Blend, 22, 72
Consonant Digraphs, 21, 94
Content, 1, 7, 8, 16, 25, 35, 50, 56, 59, 62, 63, 65, 72, 97
Content-Specific, 72
Contextual Strategies, 32
Conventional Stage, 72
Creative Writing, 52
Decoded, 25
Decoding, 7, 20, 21, 24, 27, 68, 89
Description, 54
Diction, 63
Differentiated Instruction, 45, 63
Digital Literacy, 57, 59
Digital Tools, 65
Directionality, 15
Discussion, 58, 59, 61, 62, 64

Distance Learning, 59
Drama, 50
Dynamic Characters, 50
Early Intermediate Literacy Stage, 14
Editing Step, 64
Encoding, 21, 27, 68, 89
Explicitly, 20, 25, 36, 42, 68, 69, 99
Expository, 67
Feedback, 56, 63
Figurative Language, 52, 80, 83, 97, 99
First-Person Point of View, 51
Flash Cards, 26, 30
Flat Character, 50
Fluency, 7, 29, 35, 36, 61, 62, 89
Formative Assessment, 56
Fry Graph, 30
Fry's Formula, 30, 31, 32
Graphemes, 36, 78
Graphic Organizers, 43, 46
High-Frequency Words, 35, 95
Inferential Comprehension, 53
Informational Text, 7, 40, 50, 54
Informational Writing, 67
Intermediate Literacy Stage, 14
Irregular Words, 24, 25, 26, 35, 71, 94
Kinesthetic Learning, 60
KWL Charts, 39, 43, 46, 82, 83, 99
Language Comprehension, 40
Letter Recognition, 17
Level of Meaning, 32
Lexile Text Measures, 31
Listening Comprehension, 40, 77, 96
Literal Comprehension, 53
Literary Elements, 50
Literary Nonfiction, 50
Manipulation of Syllables, 12
Morphemes, 24, 78, 94
Morphological Maps, 33
Multisensory Approach, 25
Narrative Writing, 67
Narrator, 50, 51
Non-Decodable, 25, 27, 28
Non-Print Sources, 41
One-to-One Correspondence, 15
Onset, 13

Index

Order of Importance, 54
Organize, 46
Orthography, 24
Parenthetical Elements, 32
Persuasive Text, 50
Persuasive Writing, 67
Phoneme, 13, 14, 18, 19, 36, 68, 94, 95
Phoneme Deletion, 13
Phoneme Substitution, 14
Phoneme-Grapheme Correspondence, 20
Phonemic Awareness, 7, 13, 35, 36, 68, 94, 100
Phonetic Stage, 38, 39, 69, 70, 94
Phonics Instruction, 21
Phonological Awareness, 12, 76, 95
Picture Walk, 42
Plot, 42, 43, 50, 51, 53, 67, 68
Poetry, 49, 51
Point of View, 51
Precommunicative Writing, 69
Predictable Structures, 31
Prefixes, 23, 24, 77, 94
Pre-Phonetic Stage, 76, 95
Print, 15, 16, 75, 77, 94
Print Awareness, 15, 75, 77, 94
Problem/Solution, 54
Prose, 49
Prosody, 35
Protagonist, 50
Qualitative Measures, 31
Quantitative Measures, 30
Rainbow Writing, 25
Readability Formulas, 30
Reading Comprehension, 40, 43, 78
Reading Fluency, 21, 24, 35, 36, 37, 38, 39
Reading Rate, 35
Reciprocal Phonological Skills, 20, 28
Recursively, 20
Return Sweeping, 15
Revision Step, 64
Rime, 13, 75
Root Word, 23, 96
Schwa, 22
Second Person Point of View, 51
Segmenting, 12, 68
Semantic Organizers, 14, 48
Setting, 36, 41, 42, 43, 51, 53, 67, 68
Sight Words, 24, 25, 26, 27, 28, 36, 75, 79, 94
Skim, 32, 55
Spatial Order, 54, 84
Speaker, 50, 51
Spelling Development, 69
Storyboards, 43
Structural Analysis, 24, 32, 75, 76, 77, 78, 94, 95
Suffixes, 23, 24, 77, 94
Summarize, 37, 40, 41, 42, 43, 65
Syllabic Analysis, 24, 76
Syllabication, 24
Syllables, 12, 24
Systematically, 20, 69
Teacher-Led Practice, 68
Text Evidence, 82, 98, 99
Thesis Statement, 67
Third Person Limited, 51
Third Person Omniscient, 51
Third Person Point of View, 51
Timed-Reading, 36
Timed-Repeated Readings, 36
Tone, 35, 51
Tragedy, 50
Transitional Terms, 55
Trick Words, 25
Venn Diagrams, 43, 46
Visual Aids, 46
Visual Learning, 59
Vocabulary, 7, 29, 32, 34, 36, 37, 77, 80, 89
Word Analysis, 24, 78, 82, 99
Word Families, 23
Word Maps, 32
Word Recognition, 24, 35, 36
Word Walls, 39, 70
Word Webs, 14, 33, 48
Words, 15, 23, 24, 25, 34
Worksheets, 26
Written Expression, 63

Dear Praxis Test Taker,

Thank you for purchasing this study guide for your Praxis Teaching Reading 5205 exam. We hope that we exceeded your expectations.

Our goal in creating this study guide was to cover all of the topics that you will see on the test. We also strove to make our practice questions as similar as possible to what you will encounter on test day. With that being said, if you found something that you feel was not up to your standards, please send us an email and let us know.

We would also like to let you know about other books in our catalog that may interest you.

Praxis Core

This can be found on Amazon: amazon.com/dp/1637753632/

Praxis Elementary Education Multiple Subjects

This can be found on Amazon: amazon.com/dp/1637756046/

We have study guides in a wide variety of fields. If the one you are looking for isn't listed above, then try searching for it on Amazon or send us an email.

Thanks Again and Happy Testing!
Product Development Team
info@studyguideteam.com

FREE Test Taking Tips Video/DVD Offer

To better serve you, we created videos covering test taking tips that we want to give you for FREE. **These videos cover world-class tips that will help you succeed on your test.**

We just ask that you send us feedback about this product. Please let us know what you thought about it—whether good, bad, or indifferent.

To get your **FREE videos**, you can use the QR code below or email freevideos@studyguideteam.com with "Free Videos" in the subject line and the following information in the body of the email:

    a. The title of your product

    b. Your product rating on a scale of 1-5, with 5 being the highest

    c. Your feedback about the product

If you have any questions or concerns, please don't hesitate to contact us at info@studyguideteam.com.

Thank you!